153.14 Pa
33327007
Parkinson
I before
: old-sci

D0985123

A Gift for

LIBRARY DISCARD
Presented by
NON-RETURNABLE

i before e
(except after c)

Every man's memory is his private literature.

—ALDOUS HUXLEY

i before e
(except after c)

old-school ways
to remember stuff

JUDY PARKINSON

Reader's
Digest

The Reader's Digest Association, Inc.
Pleasantville, New York/Montreal

MOOSE JAW PUBLIC LIBRARY

A READER'S DIGEST BOOK

Copyright © 2009 Michael O'Mara Books Limited

Illustrations © Louise Morgan 2007
For www.artmarketillustration.com

All rights reserved. Unauthorized reproduction, in any manner, is prohibited.

Reader's Digest is a registered trademark of The Reader's Digest Association, Inc.

First published in Great Britain in 2007 by Michael O'Mara Books Limited
9 Lion Yard, Tremadoc Road
London SW4 7NQ

FOR MICHAEL O'MARA BOOKS
Illustrations by Louise Morgan
Cover design by Angie Allison
Front cover title lettering by Toby Buchan
Interior design by Martin Bristow

FOR READER'S DIGEST
U.S. Project Staff
Project Editor: Sandra Kear
Associate Art Director: George McKeon

Canadian Project Staff
Contributing Editor: J.D. Gravenor
Proofreader: Jesse Corbeil
Senior Designer: Andrée Payette
Manager, Book Editorial: Pamela Johnson
Production Manager: Gordon Howlett
Production Coordinator: Gillian Sylvain

Reader's Digest Association (Canada) ULC
Vice President, Book Editorial: Robert Goyette

Parkinson, Judy.
    I before E : old-school ways to remember stuff / Judy Parkinson.
        p. cm.
    ISBN 978-1-55475-002 -3
1. Mnemonics--Handbooks, manuals, etc. I. Title.
    BF385.P37 2008 153.1'4--dc22

                                                                2007052006

Every effort has been made to trace and contact copyright holders of the materials
in this book. The author and publisher will be glad to rectify any omissions.

We are committed to both the quality of our products and the service we provide to
our customers. We value your comments, so please feel free to contact us.

The Reader's Digest Association (Canada) ULC
Book Editor
1100 René-Levesque Blvd. West
Montreal, QC H3B 5H5

For more Reader's Digest products and information, visit our website at **rd.ca**

Printed in the United States of America

09 10 11 12 / 5 4 3 2 1

Contents

Introduction

―――――

"Thirty days hath September, April, June, and
November..."

How many times, perhaps anxiously awaiting payday,
have you repeated this saying to yourself? Or racked your
brains for the name of Canada's longest-serving prime
minister in order to stump some impertinent know-it-all
at a dinner party?

No doubt about it, memory's a funny business. But in a
pre-Google, less hectic age, many useful, if not invaluable,
facts were taught by mnemonics—simple memory aids,
which once learned, fixed information in the brain forever.
In fact, the concept of memory devices began in ancient
Greece, before the written word. Rather than memorize
information by rote, the Greeks developed a technique
called the Method of Loci (pronounced LOW-sigh), or
method of locations or places.

With this method a person creates an image that
associates the necessary information with a location or
place along a familiar and well-travelled route. To
retrieve the items from memory, the person then mentally
travels through that visualization, picking up the
previously associated items.

As Cicero tells it in his work *De Oratore*, this method
was invented by a Greek poet named Simonides of Ceos
(c. 556-468 B.C.). After a recitation at a dinner party,
Simonides was apparently called outside. While he was

outside, the roof of the building he was in collapsed, killing all inside, many beyond recognition. Simonides was able to identify the victims by associating their names with their respective positions at the dinner table, and it is believed that through this tragedy, an ancient system of mnemonics was born.

Since then, hundreds of new mnemonic devices have been created to give knowledge seekers an advantage. Studies have shown time and again that people who use mnemonics remember at least twice as well as those who don't.

This book assembles many of the quirky and amusing methods that people have devised to remember tidbits of information in school—all of them still handy todat. Packed with clever verses, entertaining acronyms, curious—and sometimes hilarious—sayings, *i before e (except after c)* includes all the mnemonics you could ever need (and some you probably don't).

This book is your one-stop shop for finding basic mnemonics. Soon you'll be recalling them to pass a test or include in a speech. They can help remind you when to turn your clocks back and forward, as well as important anniversaries and that special someone's birthday. Mnemonics could even save you from contacting poison ivy or may help you save a life. By the end of it, you'll definitely remember *i before e* as an amusing and handy collection of ingenious mind tricks devised to help us learn and understand the idiosyncrasies of this world and beyond.

1

The English Language

━━━━━

The Alphabet

Children, of course, must first learn the alphabet before they successfully embark upon reading the complete works of Shakespeare. So it is that for many of us, learning our ABCs to the tune of "Twinkle, Twinkle, Little Star" (made famous by *Sesame Street's* Big Bird) becomes our first introduction to the world of mnemonics.

It was Charles Bradlee, a Boston music publisher, who first copyrighted that combination in 1835, calling it "the ABC, a German air with variations for flute with an easy accompaniment for the pianoforte."

> *a–b–c–d–e–f–g,*
> *h–i–j–k–l–m–n–o–p,*
> *q–r–s–t–u–v,*
> *w–x–y and z.*
> *Now I know my ABCs,*
> *next time won't you sing with me?*

For the rhyme to work with the Z, you have to use the U.S. pronunciation of zee rather than zed. If you didn't sing your ABCs to the tune of "Twinkle, Twinkle, Little Star," then you might have used the tune of "Baa, Baa, Black Sheep" instead, which has a similar rhythm and the same melody.

Because the letters l—m—n—o—p have to be sung twice as fast as the rest of the letters in the rhyme, some children have mistakenly assumed that "elemenopee" is a

word. The *Sesame Street: The Alphabet Jungle Game* DVD pokes fun at this type of error. In the video Telly thinks he's been stumped when Zoe introduces the next letter after K, called "Elemeno." After some worrisome bantering, Elmo enlightens his friends to the error, and an animated short on each letter follows, in classic *Sesame Street* style.

In the nineteenth century, a popular way to teach

children the ABCs was through a rhyme entitled "The Tragical Death of A, Apple Pie, Who Was Cut in Pieces, and Eaten by Twenty-Six Gentlemen, With Whom All Little People Ought To Be Very Well Acquainted." The text dates back as far as the reign of Charles II (1660–1685).

A was an apple pie
B bit it,
C cut it,
D dealt it,
E eats it,
F fought for it,
G got it,
H had it,
I inspected it,
J jumped for it,
K kept it,
L longed for it,
M mourned for it,
N nodded at it,
O opened it,
P peeped in it,
Q quartered it,
R ran for it,
S stole it,
T took it,
U upset it,
V viewed it,
W wanted it,
X, **Y** and **Z** all wished for
and had a piece in hand.

The Five Vowels

The English alphabet has five soft vowels: **A E I O U**. This sequence of letters generally tends to roll off the tongue quite naturally, but for anyone who has trouble remembering the order of vowels, here are a couple of useful phrases:

Ann's **E**gg **I**s **O**n **U**s.

Anthony's **E**go **I**s **O**ver **U**sed.

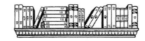

The Parts of Speech

After learning the alphabet, the next step is to devise coherent sentences. The rhyme below categorizes each of the parts of speech, giving a clear example of each grammatical term. The rhyme dates back to 1855 and was written by educators David B. Tower and Benjamin F. Tweed:

A NOUN's the name of any thing;
As, *school or garden, hoop, or swing.*

ADJECTIVES tell the kind of noun;
As, *great, small, pretty, white, or brown.*

Three of these words we often see
Called ARTICLES — *a, an,* and *the.*

Instead of nouns the PRONOUNS stand;

John's head, his face, my arm, your hand.

VERBS tell of something being done;
As, *read, write, spell, sing, jump,* or *run.*

How things are done the ADVERBS tell;
As, *slowly, quickly, ill,* or *well.*

They also tell us *where* and *when;*
As, *here,* and *there,* and *now,* and *then.*

A PREPOSITION stands *before*
A NOUN; as, *in,* or *through,* a door.

CONJUNCTIONS sentences unite;
As, kittens scratch *and* puppies bite.

The INTERJECTION shows surprise.

A different rhyme called "The Parts of Speech" is similarly concise as a reminder of the different components of the English language. The origin of these verses is unknown.

Every name is called a **noun,**
As *field* and *fountain, street* and *town.*

In place of noun the **pronoun** stands,
As *he* and *she* can clap their hands.

The **adjective** describes a thing,
As *magic* wand and *bridal* ring.

The **verb** means action, something done—
To *read,* to *write,* to *jump,* to *run.*

How things are done, the **adverbs** tell,
As *quickly, slowly, badly, well.*

The **preposition** shows relation,
As *in* the street, or *at* the station.

Conjunctions join, in many ways,
Sentences, words, *or* phrase *and* phrase.

The **interjection** cries out, "Hark!
I need an exclamation mark!"

Through poetry, we learn how each
Of these make up the **Parts of Speech.**

What's a Preposition?

To further remember the function of a preposition, insert
any word into the following sentence:

The squirrel ran____the tree.

For example, over, under, after, around, through, up,
on, to, from, by, and so forth. Other prepositions include
in, at, for, between, among, and of.

What's a Conjunction?

Conjunctions are words used to join two independent
clauses. Most people are careless with punctuation,
especially these days when shortcuts in e-mails and text
messages have become commonplace. But this FAN

BOYS mnemonic helps if you want to remember the coordinating conjunctions, of which the most important are *and*, *or*, and *but*.

FAN BOYS

For, **A**nd, **N**or, **B**ut, **O**r, **Y**et, **S**o

The Rules of Punctuation

Cecil Hartley's poem from *Principles of Punctuation* or *The Art of Pointing* (1818) reveals the old-fashioned way that people were advised on how to interpret punctuation when reading sentences out loud.

> The stops point out, with truth, the time of pause
> A sentence doth require at ev'ry clause.
> At ev'ry comma, stop while *one* you count;
> At semicolon, *two* is the amount;
> A colon doth require the time of *three*;
> The period *four*, as learned men agree.

Though it's not a verse that most grammarians would encourage these days, it does give you an idea of the difference between each type of punctuation mark.

On Commas

A cat has claws at the ends of its paws.
A comma's a pause at the end of a clause.

On Colons

The English teacher and prominent lexicographer H. W. Fowler creates a useful visual image of the job done by the colon, which he says, "delivers the goods that have been invoiced in the preceding words."

On the Exclamation Point

The following anonymously authored seventeenth-century rhyme appeared in *Treatise of Stops, Points, or Pauses, and of Notes Which Are Used in Writing and Print* (1680):

This stop denotes our Suddain Admiration,
Of what we Read, or Write, or giv Relation,
And is always cal'd an Exclamation.

Writing Stories

And when you put all these elements together to write your first novel, don't forget the main elements of storytelling:

Viewpoint
Mood
Plot
Characters
Theme
Setting

If the VMPCTS acronym doesn't roll easily off the tongue, this phrase should help to keep it firmly in mind:

Very **M**any **P**upils **C**ome **T**o **S**chool

Learning Lines

How do actors memorize scripts? Learning lines by repetition is the most obvious way, but many actors also refer to the beat of the script that is, the rhythm of the words, which actors literally tune into. Some plays are easier to learn than others. Shakespeare's texts are highly memorable because they are rich and full of puns (often extremely bawdy ones), rhymes, and alliterations.

> Whereat, with blade, with bloody blameful blade,
> He bravely breach'd his boiling bloody breast.

Another mnemonic secret of the English poetic tradition is the rhythm of the iambic pentameter. An iamb is a beat with one soft syllable and one strong syllable, and a series of five iambs forms the heartbeat of classic poetry: its familiarity makes it easy to remember, especially in the works of Shakespeare.

From *Hamlet*

To be / or not / to be / that is / the question.

From the Sonnets

Shall I / compare / thee to / a sum/mer's day?
Thou art / more love/ly and / more tem/perate:
Rough winds / do shake / the dar/ling buds / of May,
And sum/mer's lease / hath all / too short / a date.

Setting a text to a well-known tune and rhythm is a useful method of memorizing the words. Why not try singing Homer's *Odyssey*, Coleridge's "The Rime of the Ancient Mariner," or one of Shakespeare's sonnets to the tune of your favourite nursery rhyme or song? You can remember the words using a combination of rhymes, rhythms, and repetition.

English usage is sometimes more than mere taste, judgment, and education—sometimes it's sheer luck, like getting across the street.

— E. B. White

2
To Spell or Not to Spell

Although there are some people who can spell *supercalifragilisticexpialidocious* without blinking an eye, others draw blanks at the simplest word. Everyone has a different level of ability when it comes to spelling. For those who fall into the latter category, perhaps they weren't taught the right sort of spelling mnemonics...

I before E (except after C)

Teachers often drum this phrase into children's heads in grammar school, and it does apply in the sentence: "Receive a Piece of Pie." But all rules invariably have exceptions, just to make life difficult:

> *i* before *e*, except after *c*
> or when sounded like *a*
> as in *neighbour* and *weigh.*

A similar version ends with the line: "as in *weigh, neigh,* or *sleigh.*" Numerous exceptions to the rule include the words *neither, height, leisure,* and *weird.*

A rhyme with an extended rule used more commonly in British schools clarifies things a little further:

> When the sound is *ee*
> It's *i* before *e* except after *c*.

However, even the extended rule has a number of exceptions: words such as *caffeine, protein*, and *seize* are *e* before *i* despite having a long *ee* sound. Also, the plurals of *−cy* words end with *−cies*, which is another exception to this *i* before *e* rule, as are many *−cie* words, such as *science* and *conscience*.

Therefore, another addendum has been applied to the original saying:

> *i* before *e*, except after *c*
> Or when sounding like *a*
> As in *neighbour* and *weigh*.
> Drop this rule when *-c* sounds as *-sh*.

Words such as *ancient, efficient*, and *species* become covered by this additional rule.

The Complexities of English Spelling

The English language is full of convolutions and contradictions, which can make the spelling and pronunciations of certain words difficult to predict. This poem by Vivian Buchan, which appeared in the American National Education Association's *NEA Journal* in 1966/67, expresses the idiosyncrasies and frustrations with so-called spelling rules.

Phony Phonetics

One reason why I cannot spell,
Although I learned the rules quite well
Is that some words like *coup* and *through*
Sound just like *threw* and *flue* and *Who;*
When *oo* is never spelled the same,
The *duice* becomes a guessing game;
And then I ponder over *though,*
Is it spelled *so,* or *throw,* or *beau,*
And *bough* is never *bow,* it's *bow,*
I mean the *bow* that sounds like *plow,*
And not the *bow* that sounds like *row*—
The *row* that is pronounced like *roe.*
I wonder, too, why *rough* and *tough,*
That sound the same as *gruff* and *muff,*
Are spelled like *bough* and *though,* for they
Are both pronounced a different way.
And why can't I spell *trough* and *cough*
The same as I do *scoff* and *golf?*

[14]

Why isn't *drought* spelled just like *route,*
or *doubt* or *pout* or *sauerkraut?*
When words all sound so much the same
To change the spelling seems a shame.
There is no sense—see sound like cents—
in making such a difference
Between the sight and sound of words;
Each spelling rule that undergirds
The way a word should look will fail
And often prove to no avail
Because exceptions will negate
The truth of what the rule may state;
So though I try, I still despair
And moan and mutter "It's not fair
That I'm held up to ridicule
And made to look like such a fool
When it's the spelling that's at fault.
Let's call this nonsense to a halt."

Commonly Misspelled Words

It has almost become cliché among educators and
orthographers (who study spelling) to misspell the word
misspell in order to prove a point. It does, however,
demonstrate how easily words can run astray. You need
only do an Internet search of the misspelled word
equiptment to see how poor spelling has become
commonplace.

Their/They're/There

Instructors and editors often find errors with this group of words because they're all pronounced the same but spelled differently. The possessive is *their*, and the contraction of "they are" is *they're*. Everywhere else, it is *there*. Think directions for *there*: it's either *here* or *there*. The word *here* can be found in *there*. Think of ownership for *their*: children are *heirs* before they inherit *their* fortune. If there is an *i* in it, then it is the one that refers to people.

Principal/Principle

Remember the following spelling principle: the school *principal* is a *prince* and a *pal* (despite what you may think of him or her). The *principal's principle* dictates: a *principle* is a rule!

Lay and Lie

As a rule, irregular verbs pose problems for people who like neat, cut-and-dried methods to live and learn by. One forms the past and past participle of regular verbs by adding -*d* or -*ed* to the stem of the infinitive *(touch, touched)*, but this process does not apply to irregular verbs such as *lie*. So just remember the phrase:

You'll lay an egg if you don't lie down.

Affect or Effect?

The RAVEN mnemonic is useful when working out whether to use *affect* or *effect* in a sentence:

Remember: **A**ffect, **V**erb, **E**ffect, **N**oun

The woman was *affected* by the *effect* of the film.

A Useful Selection of Spelling Aids

Many of the words in the following list appear to have no logical spelling rule whatsoever, but reciting the clever mnemonic phrase that accompanies the word may help keep you out of the dunce's chair.

Accelerator
A Cruel **C**reature—imagine words and pictures to remind you to write two *c*s.

Acceptable
Remember to accept any table offered, and you will spell this word correctly.

Accessible
—able or –ible?
Say out loud, "**I** am always access**i**ble."

Accidentally
Two *c*s and an ally. Make up a story:
Two cats accidentally scratched your friend and ally.

Accommodation
Again two *c*s and two *m*s,
And don't forget that second *o* after the second *m*.
Comfortable **C**hairs, **O**r **M**odern **M**ats, **O**r…

Address
Directly **D**elivered letters are **S**afe and **S**ound.

Aeroplane
All **E**ngines **R**unning **O**kay.

Almond
ALmonds are ov**AL**s.

Amateur
Amateurs need not be mature.

Argument
A Rude **G**irl **U**ndresses—**M**y **E**yes **N**eed **T**aping.

(Another way to check your spelling is to find short words within. Think of chewing GUM when you chew over an arGUMent.)

Arithmetic
A Rat **I**n **T**he **H**ouse **M**ay **E**at **T**he **I**ce **C**ream.

A Rude **I**nterloper **T**hought **H**e **M**ight **E**at **T**urkey **I**n **C**hurch.

Assassination

This word is comprised of four short words:

Ass Ass I Nation.

Asthma

The cause of Asthm**A**:

Sensitivity **T**o **H**ousehold **M**ites.

Autumn

There's an *n* at the end of autumn.

Think of *n* standing for November, because it's the end of autumn and the beginning of winter.

Bare or Bear

Imagine scenarios relating to the two words.

It's bath time with a bar of soap on your bare skin.

A bear is scary and fills you with fear.

Beautiful

Big **E**lephants **A**re **U**sually **BEAU**tiful.

Because

Big **E**lephants **C**an **A**lways **U**nderstand **S**mall **E**lephants.

Big **E**lephants **C**an't **A**lways **U**se **S**mall **E**xits.

Believe

This word obeys the *i* before *e* rule, and there's also a perfect word association within.

Do you be**LIE**ve a **LIE**?

Biscuit

Some believe this word is derived from two French words—*bis cuit* meaning twice cooked. The easy way to remember how to spell it is with this phrase:

BIScuits are **C**rumbled **U**p **I**nto **T**iny pieces.

Broccoli

We know it's healthy, but it's tricky to spell.

Remember that broccoli would never **C**ause **COLI**c.

Calendar

Just remember that this word has an *e* between two *a*s. The last vowel is *a*.

Capital or Capitol

The capit**A**l city of Greece is **A**thens.

P**A**ris is the capital of Fr**A**nce.

Most capit**O**l buildings have d**O**mes.

There's a capit**O**l in Washingt**O**n.

Chaos
Cyclones, **H**urricanes **A**nd **O**ther **S**torms create chaos.

Character
CHARlie's **ACT** is **ER**otic.

Committee
Remember: **M**any **M**eetings **T**ake **T**ime— **E**veryone's **E**xhausted!

Conscience
It's not pronounced how it's spelled.

It's **S**cience with **C**on at the beginning.

Consensus
The census does not require a consensus, since they are not related.

Correspondence
CORRect your **CORR**espon**DEN**ce in the **DEN**.

Definitely
Find the word **FINITE** within.

Deliberate
It was a de**LIBERATE** plan to **LIBERATE** the hostages.

Desert (as in the Sahara) or Dessert (as in apple pie)
Remember that the sweet one has two **S**ugar**S**.

Or that the double *s* in dessert stands for "sweet stuff."

Diarrhea
If you need to know how to spell this—here you go!

Dash **I**n **A** **R**eal **R**ush—**H**urriedly **E**vading **A**ccident.

Doubt

Sometimes it's only natural to **B**e in doubt.

Dumbbell

Even smart people forget one of the *b*s in this one. (So be careful whom you call one when you write.)

Eccentric

The word literally means "off centre," so imagine an eccentric **C**razy **C**at, running around in circles.

Eczema

It's pronounced with an *x*, but there's no X-factor with this problem:

Even **C**lean **ZE**alots **MA**y get eczema.

Embarrass

Do you turn **R**eally **R**ed **A**nd **S**mile **S**hyly when embarrassed?

Exaggerate

If he's br**AGG**ing, then he's surely exaggerating.

Fascinate

Are you fa**SCI**nated by **SCI**ence?

Fiery

The silent *e* on fire is so cowardly: it retreats inside the word rather than face the suffix *-y*.

Forty

FORget the *u* in four when you spell **FOR**ty.

Friend

FRIEs are for sharing with your **FRIE**nd.

Geography

General **E**isenhower's **O**ldest **G**irl **R**ode **A** **P**ony **H**ome **Y**esterday.

Grammar

There's no *e* in grammar.

Think about Grand**MA**, who teaches perfect grammar.

Grateful

You should be grateful to know that keeping "great" out of "grateful" is great.

Handkerchief

It's shortened to "hanky," but the long form has a *d*.

Think of holding a handkerchief in your **HAND**.

Heard or Herd

If you heard something, you used your **EAR**.

There are lots of animals in a herd, so there can't be a single one on its own in this word.

Indispensable

Only the most **ABLE** are indispens**ABLE**.

Interrupt

It's a fact that it's **R**eally **R**ude to interrupt.

Liaison

Dangerous and often misspelled.

To spot a liaison, use your two eyes (*2 l*s).

Lightning

Lighten the load of the word lightning by learning how to eliminate the *e*.

Memento

Commonly misspelled as "momento."

A souvenir from your holiday is a memento, and it represents happy **MEM**ories.

Millennium

A thousand years—**MILLE**—that's more than Ninety-**N**ine years.

Miniature

It means tiny, and there are tiny words in the middle—*i* and *a*.

Misspell

The subject of this section of the book.

Don't mi**SS** that extra *s* in **MiSS**pell.

Necessary

Not **E**very **C**at **E**ats **S**ardines—**S**ome **A**re **R**eally **Y**ummy.

Or think of a shirt—it is necessary for a shirt to have one **C**ollar and two **S**leeve**S**.

Or think of your necessary coffee each morning with one **C**ream and two **S**ugar**S**.

Occasion

If it's a special one, you'd travel over two seas (*c*s).

Ocean

Only **C**at's **E**yes **A**re **N**arrow.

Parallel

There are three *l*s in parallel, but think of the middle ones acting as parallel lines next to each other.

Parliament

Think: **I AM** parliament.

People

People **E**at **O**ther **P**eople's **L**eftovers **E**agerly.

Pneumonia

People **N**ever **E**xpect **U**s to come down with **PNEU**monia.

Possession

Very sweet—four **S**ugar**S**.

Potassium

One **T**ea and two **S**ugar**S**.

Recommend

No need for confusion with this word. It's simply commend with *re-* at the beginning.

Rhythm

Rhythm **H**elps **Y**ou **T**o **H**ear **M**usic.

Rhythm **H**elps **Y**our **T**wo **H**ips **M**ove.

Separate
The *e*s surround the *a*s.

Or think of your old Father or **PA** in his den as a se**PA**rate kind of person.

Stationery or Stationary
A or *e*? Every office intern gets the spelling of this word wrong at least once in his or her life. You only have to remember one, and by process of elimination, the other one must be right. Think of the initial *e* in envelope for stationery, or keep in mind the following sentences:

PEns are items of stationery.

CArs when parked are stationary.

Subtle
To **B**e subtle—**B**e silent.

Succeed
Succeed, **P**roceed, **E**xceed are the only three English words that end in **CEED**.

Take the initial letters of these words and think **SPEED**.

Together

Split it up into three separate words:

To get her.

Weather or Whether

WE look **AT HER** (the TV weather girl) to check the forecast and discover whether it will be sunny or rainy.

Wednesday

WE Do **N**ot **E**at **S**oup **D**ay.

Weird

Weird doesn't follow the *i* before *e* rule, because weird is just weird.

You're or Your

YOU'RE never going to get it right if you don't use **YOUR** head.

If something belongs to us, it is **OUR**s, just as something that belongs to you is **YOUR**s.

Eye halve a spelling checker
It came with my pea sea
It plainly marques for my revue
Miss steaks eye kin knot sea.

Eye strike a key and type a word
And weight four it to say
Weather eye am wrong oar write
It shows me strait a weigh.

As soon as a mist ache is maid
It nose bee fore two long
And eye can put the error rite
It's rare lea ever wrong.

Eye have run this poem threw it
Eye am shore your pleased two no
It's letter perfect awl the weigh
My checker tolled me sew.

—Margo Roark

www.spellingsociety.org/news/media/poems.php

3
Think of a Number

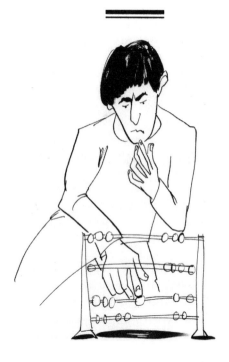

First Steps: Counting Rhymes

Learning to count is the first step to understanding arithmetic. Most children learn counting by reciting nursery rhymes, which contain the essential ingredients of mnemonics: imagery, rhyme, and fun. "One, Two, Buckle My Shoe" was devised many years ago as a fun way to teach children how to count to 20 using visual language and repetitive rhythm. Here are two slightly different versions of the famous verse:

> One, Two, buckle my shoe,
> Three, Four, knock at the door,
> Five, Six, pick up sticks,
> Seven, Eight, lay them straight,
> Nine, Ten, a big fat hen,
> Eleven, Twelve, dig and delve,
> Thirteen, Fourteen, maids a-courting,
> Fifteen, Sixteen, maids in the kitchen,
> Seventeen, Eighteen, maids in waiting,
> Nineteen, Twenty, my plate's empty.

> One, Two, buckle my shoe,
> Three, Four, knock at the door,
> Five, Six, pick up sticks,
> Seven, Eight, don't be late,
> Nine, Ten, a good fat hen,
> Eleven, Twelve, dig and delve
> Thirteen, Fourteen, maids a-courting,
> Fifteen, Sixteen, maids a-kissing,
> Seventeen, Eighteen, maids a-waiting,
> Nineteen, Twenty, I've had plenty.

"One, Two, Three, Four, Five," also known as "Once I Caught a Fish Alive," is another famous counting rhyme. Though its origins are unknown, its earliest date of publication has been traced back to 1888:

> One, two, three, four, five.
> Once I caught a fish alive.
> Six, seven, eight, nine, ten.
> Then I let it go again.
> Why did you let it go?
> Because it bit my finger so.
> Which finger did it bite?
> This little finger on my right.

This shorter counting rhyme was also popular with children:

> One, Two, Three, Four,
> Mary's at the cottage door.
> Five, Six, Seven, Eight,
> Eating cherries off a plate.

Writing Numbers

Mastering numbers out loud is one thing, but writing them down is something else entirely. However, the number-writing poem on the next page doubtless helped countless youngsters.

Around to the left to find my hero,
Back to the top, I've made a zero.

Downward stroke; my, that's fun,
Now I've made the number 1.

Half a heart says, "I love you."
A line—now I made the number 2.

Around the tree, around the tree,
Now I've made the number 3.

Down, across and down once more
Now I've made the number 4.

The hat, the back, the belly—a 5.
Watch out! It might come alive.

Bend down low to pick up sticks,
Now I've made the number 6.

Across the sky, and down from heaven,
Now I've made the number 7.

Make an *s* and close the gate,
Now I've made the number 8.

An oval and a line,
Now I've made the number 9.

One (1) egg (0) laid my hen.
Now I've made the number 10.

Roman Numerals

Imagine doing sums using Roman numerals. They are still used today for indicating successive same-name successors to kings and queens, as well as for movie sequels, Olympic Games, and the Super Bowl, but their usage is quite rare. I, V, and X are more commonly used, particularly on clock and watch faces, making it more familiar that they represent 1, 5, and 10 respectively. It's a good idea to remember that C stands for "century," i.e., 100 years:

I	V	X	L	C	D	M
1	5	10	50	100	500	1,000

The Romans did not have a notation for zero, which meant that early in the second millennium the system was gradually replaced by the Arabic numerals used today. Modern society rarely uses Roman numerals anymore; there's a danger that this system may become obsolete. This simple mnemonic helps keep the numerals in order:

I Value **X**ylophones **L**ike **C**ows **D**ig **M**ilk.

Remember the first three letters IVX, then recite the following to recall LCD and M:

Lucy **C**an't **D**rink **M**ilk.

The poem on the next page provides a rhythmic visual image for learning Roman numerals.

X shall stand for playmates Ten,
V for Five stout stalwart men,
I for One as I'm alive,
C for Hundred and D for Five,
M for a Thousand soldiers true,
And L for Fifty, I'll tell you.

As is this brief yet concise verse:

M's mille—or 1,000 said,
D's half—500 quickly read.
C's just a 100—century
And L is half again—50.
So all that's left is X and V
Or 10 and 5 and I is easy.

The Metric System

Metrication, or the decimal system, began in France in the 1790s. Canada adopted the metric system gradually, starting in the 1970s. Soft drinks and gasoline are sold in litres; dental floss is measured in metres; and long before the digital age, 35-mm film was a popular standard format. If you're still confused, don't worry, get metrified. Here are some clever mnemonics to help you make sense of the metric system. Don't despair. If all else fails, use one of the many metric conversion calculators available on the Internet.

Kilometre	1,000 metres
Hectometre	100 metres
Decametre	10 metres
Metre (base)	1 metre
Decimetre	¹⁄₁₀ of a metre
Centimetre	¹⁄₁₀₀ of a metre
Millimetre	¹⁄₁₀₀₀ of a metre

The first letters stand for the metric prefixes and base unit: Kilo, Hecto, Deca, Metre (base), Deci, Centi, Milli. The following phrases help to remember the correct order:

King **H**enry **D**ied **M**ightily **D**rinking **C**hocolate **M**ilk

Keep **H**er **D**iamond **M**ine **D**own **C**reek, **M**ister

King **H**enry **D**ied—**M**other **D**idn't **C**are **M**uch

King **H**ector **D**ied **M**iserable **D**eath—**C**aught **M**easles

If the base unit is a gram rather than a metre we would have:

King **H**enry **D**ied—**G**ranny **D**idn't **C**are **M**uch

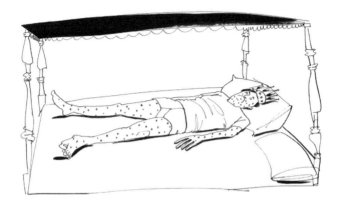

Times-Table Tricks

Ten Times-table

When multiplying a number by 10, add a zero to it. This is a simple mnemonic device— 3 × 10 = 30, just as 26,350 × 10 = 263,500. As the numbers get larger, add a zero and move the comma to the right by one place.

Nine Times-table

The study of arithmetic presents an infinite number of patterns to discover. One involves the nine times-table.

9 × 1 = 9	9 × 6 = 54
9 × 2 = 18	9 × 7 = 63
9 × 3 = 27	9 × 8 = 72
9 × 4 = 36	9 × 9 = 81
9 × 5 = 45	9 × 10 = 90

Notice that the product of 9 × 5 inverts at 9 × 6 to 54:

$$9 \times 5 = 45; 9 \times 6 = 54$$

Also, up to 9 × 10, the digits in the products of numbers multiplied by 9 always add up to 9:

$$9 \times 2 = 18 \ (1 + 8 = 9), 9 \times 3 = 27 \ (2 + 7 = 9).$$

Nine Times-table: By Hand

Many people learned this clever way to remember our nine times-table.

First, hold your two hands up with the palms facing you, and number each digit from 1 to 10, starting with the thumb on your left hand (1) through to the thumb on your right hand (10).

For 9 × 2, you need to bend digit number 2 (your left index finger) to signify *times 2*. This leaves your thumb (1) outstretched to the left of your bent index finger, and 8 digits outstretched to the right of it. Put 1 and 8 together to form the product of 9 × 2.

For 9 × 6, you need to bend digit number 6 (your right pinky) to represent *times 6*. This leaves all the digits on your left hand outstretched (5) and the remaining digits on your right hand outstretched (4). Put 5 and 4 together to make the product of 9 × 6.

The key involves looking at the number of fingers to the left side of the folded-down finger to find the number for the tens column of the answer, and looking to the right of the folded-down finger to find the number for the ones column.

More Times-table Tricks

Eight Times-table
8 × 8 fell on the floor, when I picked it up, it was 64!
8 and 9 are nice, but I like seven, too (72).

Seven Times-table
Three 7s had drinks and fun, and so they must be 21.
7 × 7 were in a mine, it must be 1849.

Six Times-table
6 and 7 went on a date and secured a table four two (42).

Five Times-table
Learn to count by fives, and remember that the products always end with a 5 or an 0.

Four Times-table
To 4 × 4 it would seem, long ago was sweet 16.

Three Times-table
Three cats have nine lives before heaven, until they turn 27.

Two Times-table
To multiply by two is great; it must end in 0, 2, 4, 6 or 8.

Long Division

When it comes to the technique for remembering which steps to follow when doing long division—**D**ivide, **M**ultiply, **S**ubtract, **B**ring down—use one of these memorable phrases:

Dad, **M**om, **S**ister, **B**rother.
Dead **M**onkeys **S**mell **B**ad.

The Order of Calculation

The order to work out a sum is: **M**ultiply and **D**ivide before you **A**dd and **S**ubtract. Any mathematical statement with an "equals" sign is an equation; that is, one side of the equation equals the other side. For example, $1 + 1 = 2$ is an equation, just as $2 \times 10 = 4 \times 5$ is an equation.

Some people find that the following phrase helps them remember the MDAS correct order:

My **D**ear **A**unt **S**ally

When things get more complicated and several functions become necessary to solve for the sum, the PEMDAS order tackles the problem:

Parentheses   **E**xponents   **M**ultiplication
Division   **A**ddition   **S**ubtraction

Certain phrases are useful for keeping the correct order in mind:

Please **E**xcuse **M**y **D**ear **A**unt **S**ally.

Please **E**xecute **M**y **D**og **A**nd **S**oon.

Put **E**very **M**an **D**own **A**nd **S**hout.

The **BIDMAS** acronym offers another alternative, but works in exactly the same way:

Brackets   **I**ndices   **D**ivision   **M**ultiplication
Addition   **S**ubtraction

BIDMAS allows you to calculate the sum written as:

$$(8 - 3) \times 4 + \frac{15}{5} - 3 = 20$$

The B for Brackets in BIDMAS means the same as the P for Parentheses in PEMDAS, as does the I for Indices and the E for Exponents. The order of Division and Multiplication is flexible, so the order can either be DM or MD.

Finding Averages

Here is an excellent way to remember the names of the four methods of finding averages, using the **Medium-Range Mean Model** method:

Median—the number exactly in the middle when a set of numbers is listed in order.

Range—the difference between the highest and lowest numbers in a set.

Mean—the sum of a set of numbers, divided by the number of numbers in the set.

Mode—the number (or numbers) that appears most frequently in a set.

Isosceles Triangles

To help distinguish between an isosceles triangle and all other types of triangles, this song sung to the tune of "Oh, Christmas Tree" proved invaluable:

> Oh, isosceles, oh, isosceles,
> Two angles have
> Equal degrees.
> Oh, isosceles, oh, isosceles,
> You look just like
> A Christmas tree.

Dividing by Fractions

A fraction is a numerical quantity that is not a whole number, for example ½ or $^{19}\!/_{20}$, which are quantities that form part of a whole.

The definition of a fraction is a numerator divided by a denominator, but which is which?

Think of "New Delhi":

NUmerator **U**p, **D**enominator **D**own.

Therefore, in ½, 1 is the numerator, 2 is the denominator.

In $^{19}/_{20}$, 19 is the numerator, 20 is the denominator.

This rhyme will help every student who gets into a muddle when dividing by fractions:

> The number you're dividing by,
> Turn upside down and multiply.

> e.g., 10 divided by $\frac{1}{2}$ = 10 × $\frac{2}{1}$ = 20
> or 15 divided by $\frac{1}{5}$ = 15 × $\frac{5}{1}$ = 75

The Value of Pi

Pi is the Greek letter π. It is a mathematical constant and calculated as the ratio of the circumference of a circle to its diameter. Pi is the number 3.14159, although in reality, it has an infinite number of decimal places.

The traditional way to remind yourself of the decimals is to use phrases containing word-length mnemonics, where the number of letters in each word corresponds to a digit.

Pi to six decimal places is:

> How I wish I could calculate pi = 3.141592

And to 14 places:

> How I like a drink,
> alcoholic of course,
> after the heavy lectures involving
> quantum mechanics = 3.14159265358979

And here's a rhyme to 20 decimal places of pi:

> Now, I wish I could recollect pi.
> "Eureka," cried the great inventor.
> Christmas Pudding, Christmas Pie,
> Is the problem's very centre.
> = 3.14159265358979323846

And to 31 decimal places:

> Sir, I bear a rhyme excelling
> In mystic force, and magic spelling
> Celestial sprites elucidate
> All my own striving can't relate
> Or locate they who can cogitate
> And so finally terminate. Finis.
> = 3.1415926535897932384626433832795

Unfortunately, this useful method of remembering pi only works up to 31 decimal places, because the thirty-second number after the decimal point is 0.

Omni, the celebrated science magazine of the late 1970s and early 1980s, devised this fun verse to help students calculate the circumference of a circle using pi:

> If you cross a circle with a line,
> Which hits the centre and runs from spine to spine,
> And the line's length is d
> The circumference will be d times 3.14159.

The area of a circle is calculated as $\pi \times r$ squared (where r is the radius) = πr^2.

To help remember the formula, think:

Apple Pie Are Square.

The circumference of a circle is calculated as $\pi \times d$ (where d is the diameter) = πd.

One memorable way to recall the formula is to think:

Cherry Pie Delicious.

The following rhyme helps teach the difference between circumference and area:

Fiddlededum, fiddlededee,
A ring round the moon is π times d.
If a hole in your sock you want repaired,
You use the formula πr squared.

Square Roots

Just as subtraction is the opposite of addition and division is the opposite of multiplication, so square roots are the opposite of squaring; that is, multiplying a number by itself, so the square root of 4 is 2 (i.e., $2 \times 2 = 4$).

This example shows a perfect square root and is therefore quite simple. Things get more interesting when math instructors explore more complicated concepts, such as the square root of 2. Which number multiplied by itself makes 2? It's not a round number, and so, as with pi, the length of each word in the following rhyme represents each digit:

> For the square root of 2,
> I wish I knew
> 1.414—the root of two.
>
> For the square root of 3,
> O, charmed was he
> 1.732—to know the root of three.
>
> For the square root of 5,
> So we now strive
> 2.236—to know the root of five.
>
> For the square root of 6,
> We need more logistics
> 2.449—to know the root of six.

Pythagoras's Theorem

Pythagoras (c. 580–500 B.C.) was a Greek mathematician and philosopher from Samos, sometimes known as the "Father of Numbers." His famous theorem is a math standard that reveals how to calculate the lengths of the three sides of a right-angled triangle.

In essence, Pythagoras's theorem states that the

square of the hypotenuse is equal to the sum of the squares of the other two sides, or HYPOTENUSE squared = BASE squared + HEIGHT squared.

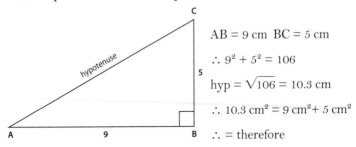

AB = 9 cm BC = 5 cm

$\therefore 9^2 + 5^2 = 106$

hyp = $\sqrt{106}$ = 10.3 cm

$\therefore$ 10.3 cm² = 9 cm²+ 5 cm²

$\therefore$ = therefore

To help math students remember the formula, a visual aid in the form of fairy tale romance was devised, which features a memorable mnemonic punch line:

Three dashing squires were courting the same princess. One squire wore a coat made from a hippopotamus hide. The second wore a bear hide. The third wore a buffalo hide. The princess told the squires that she would marry the one who cold provide the finest gift within one year. The squire with the bear hide set off and built her a castle. The squire with the buffalo hide built her a chapel. But the squire with the hippopotamus hide managed to build her a castle *and* a chapel, thus winning her hand. And the moral of the story?

The squire in the hippopotamus is equal to the sum of the squires in the other two hides.

Trigonometry: Sine Cosine Tangent

By definition, triangles are all about threes—sides and angles. If you know two elements of a right-angled triangle—whether it be sides, angles, or one of each—you can then calculate the third.

In a right-angled triangle, if the value of a second angle is given:

the **S**ine of the angle = the ratio of the **O**pposite side to the **H**ypotenuse

the **C**osine of the angle = the ratio of the **A**djacent side to the **H**ypotenuse

the **T**angent of the angle = the ratio of the **O**pposite and the **A**djacent sides

For example, in this diagram:

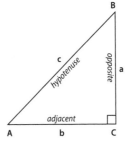

$$\sin(A) = \frac{a}{c}$$

$$\cos(A) = \frac{b}{c}$$

$$\tan(A) = \frac{a}{b}$$

The initials spell **SOH–CAH–TOA**, which is easy to recall because it rhymes with Krakatoa, the volcanic island in Indonesia. If, however, the volcano comparison is less than effective, one of the examples on the next page might prove more memorable.

Smiles **Of** **H**appiness **C**ome
After **H**aving **T**ankards **Of** **A**le.

Some **O**ld **H**ag **C**aught
A **H**ippy **T**ripping **O**n **A**cid.

Some **O**ld **H**orse **C**aught **A**nother **H**orse
Taking **O**ats **A**way.

Graph Coordinates

From simple bar charts showing hours of sunshine against months of the year to advanced calculus graphs indicating rates of change, this is the rule for all graphs:

X along the corridor,
Y up and down the stairs.

The convention for labeling a pair of coordinates (x and y) is that x is the horizontal axis and y the vertical axis.

Converting Miles to Kilometres

Fibonacci numbers are named after the thirteenth-century mathematician Leonardo of Pisa, who was also called Leonardo Fibonacci. They are whole numbers in sequence: 0, 1, 2, 3, 5, 8, 13, 21, 34, 55, 89 . . . and so on to infinity. Each number in the series is the sum of the previous two numbers.

There are approximately 8 (8.05 km) kilometres in 5 miles, and since both 8 and 5 are Fibonacci numbers, you can convert kilometres to miles and miles to kilometres by looking at the consecutive numbers. Just remember, there will always be more kilometres (longer word) than miles (shorter word).

$$8 \text{ km} = 5 \text{ miles}$$
$$13 \text{ km} = 8 \text{ miles}$$
$$21 \text{ km} = 13 \text{ miles}$$
$$34 \text{ km} = 21 \text{ miles}$$
$$55 \text{ km} = 34 \text{ miles}$$
$$89 \text{ km} = 55 \text{ miles}$$

The hardest arithmetic to master is that which enables us to count our blessings.

—Eric Hoffer
Reflections on the Human Condition

4

Geographically
Speaking

Learning Directions

The four cardinal directions (north, south, east, and west) form the introduction to many geography lessons. Remembering exactly where these points fall on a compass should be quite straightforward, but to avoid memory loss, a number of useful phrases have been devised.

Consider, for example, the acronym NEWS:

North at the top
East on the right
West on the left
South at the bottom

Alternatively, the first letter of each word in these sentences indicates the points of the compass in clockwise order:

Never **E**at **S**hredded **W**heat.

Never **E**at **S**limy **W**orms.

Never **E**nter **S**anta's **W**orkshop.

Never **E**at **S**oggy **W**affles.

Naughty **E**lephants **S**quirt **W**ater.

Latitude and Longitude

If you've ever had problems remembering the direction of latitude and longitude lines, here are a few mnemonic pointers to ensure you won't get lost.

The Latin word *latus* means "side"; hence, latitude lines go from side to side.

The phrase "Lat is fat" should help remind us that the central lines of latitude go around the "belt" of the equator.

*Long*itude lines seem *long*er, going from top to bottom or north to south.

The Tropics of Cancer and Capricorn

These are two imaginary lines running parallel to the equator (the longest line of latitude that spans the center of the globe), which are based on the sun's position in relation to the earth at two points of the year. The sun is directly overhead at noon on the Tropic of Cancer on June 21 (the beginning of summer in the Northern Hemisphere and of winter in the Southern Hemisphere) and is again overhead at midday on the Tropic of Capricorn on December 21 (the beginning of winter in the Northern Hemisphere and of summer in the Southern Hemisphere).

The Tropic of Cancer lies 23.5° north of the equator and the Tropic of Capricorn lies at 23.5° south, and the following verse has helped many to remember this fact.

CaNcer lies North of the equator.
CapricOrn lies on the Other side of the equator.

Map Reading

Imagine you're a Girl Scout or Boy Scout on an expedition carrying no more than a chocolate bar and a topographical map, or a soldier in the field armed with just a map and a compass. Your map grid reference is 123456. To find your position on the map just think: "Onward and Upward."

Split your map reference into two sets of three figures: 123 and 456.

The 1 is the number of the grid line on the map going across—ONWARD—from west to east. The 2 and 3 give more precise coordinates within that grid.

The 4 is the grid line going up—UPWARD—from south to north. And the 5 and 6 give a more precise location.

The Seven Continents of the World

A continent is defined as a large continuous landmass, and geographers state that the world has seven of them:

Europe Asia Africa Australia
Antarctica North America South America

Although Europe is joined to Asia, the two areas are recognized as separate continents, with the Ural Mountains in Russia dividing the areas that we regard as East and West. Australia is the smallest continent and is also known as Oceania. Australia itself is an island of just under 3 million square miles. Asia is the largest continent at approximately 17 million square miles.

The following phrases are the most popular to remember the continents:

Eat **A**n **A**spirin **A**fter **A** **N**asty **S**andwich.
Eat **A**n **A**pple **A**s **A** **N**ice **S**nack.

The Five Oceans

For a long time, geography teachers categorized four oceans when teaching about the 70 to 75 percent of the earth that is blanketed with water. But in the spring of 2000, the International Hydrographic Organization officially established the Southern Ocean as number five, defining its often frozen perimeters. Now students need to memorize five oceans: Pacific, Atlantic, Indian, Southern, and Arctic (from largest to smallest). Form your own mnemonic to remember the PAISA acronym, such as:

Pacifiers **A**re **I**cky, **S**omeone **A**ttested.

Pick **A**n **I**ndian **S**ummer **A**pple.

The Great Lakes

The five Great Lakes from west to east are: **S**uperior, **M**ichigan, **H**uron, **E**rie, and **O**ntario. As SMHEO is a less than memorable acronym, these short pithy sentences are far more effective:

> **S**ally **M**ade **H**enry **E**at **O**nions.
> **S**he **M**akes **H**im **E**at **O**reos.
> **S**uper **M**ario **H**eaved **E**arth **O**ut.

From east to west, try:

> **O**ld **E**lephants **H**ave **M**uch **S**kin.

An easier and more commonly used mnemonic acronym is HOMES, but this scrambles the correct geographical order.

Niagara Falls

Use the letters LENOR as a reminder of which two Great Lakes surround Niagara Falls. Picture the scene as if looking at a map where north is at the top of the page:

> **L**eft—**E**rie—**N**iagara—**O**ntario—**R**ight

Mexico and Central America

There are eight Central American countries, namely: **M**exico, **G**uatemala, **B**elize, **H**onduras, **E**l Salvador, **N**icaragua, **C**osta Rica and **P**anama. If these names or the letters MGBHENCP don't roll easily off your tongue, try using this mnemonic phrase to jog your memory:

My **G**reat **B**ig **H**ungry **E**lephant
Nearly **C**onsumed **P**anama.

The World's Longest Rivers

An unusual acronym used to remember the names of the world's longest rivers is NAYY CLAIM. The exact length of the two greatest rivers on Earth—the Nile and the Amazon—varies over time, and geographers disagree on their actual length. Therefore, this acronym is more of an aid to remembering the names of the rivers, rather than their exact pecking order, about which no one seems able to agree. In fact, this list changes significantly when all tributaries are included.

River	Continent	Length
Nile	Africa	6,695 km (4,160 miles)
Amazon	South America	6,683 km (4,150 miles)
Yangtze (Chang Jiang)	Asia	6,380 km (3,964 miles)
Yellow (Huang He)	Asia	4,830 km (3,000 miles)
Congo (Zaire)	Africa	4,630 km (2,880 miles)
Lena	Asia	4,400 km (2,734 miles)
Amur (Heilong Jiang)	Asia	4,350 km (2,703 miles)
Irtysh	Asia	4,248 km (2,640 miles)
Mekong	Asia	4,180 km (2,600 miles)

The three longest rivers in North America, including tributaries, can be recalled using the acronym MMR (think Measles, Mumps, and Rubella):

River	Country of Origin	Length
Mississippi-Missouri	United States	5,970 km (3,709 miles)
Mackenzie	Canada	4,240 km (2,635 miles)
Rio Grande	United States and Mexico	3,034 km (1,885 miles)

The Seven Hills of Rome

Rome was built on the seven hills east of the Tiber River. Clockwise from the westernmost hill, they are **C**apitoline, **Q**uirinal, **V**iminal, **E**squiline, **C**aelian, **A**ventine and **P**alatine, and they can be easily remembered with the following phrase:

Can **Q**ueen **V**ictoria **E**at **C**old **A**pple **P**ie?

Alternatively, if you start with the Quirinal, going in a clockwise direction, you could try remembering a slightly more amusing alternative:

Queen **V**ictoria **E**yes **C**aesar's **A**wfully **P**ainful **C**orns.

An even more memorable acronym is **PACE QVC**. *Pace*, the Italian word for "peace," is paired with QVC, the shopping channel.

Italian Geography

If you ever need a reminder of the location of Sicily, here's a verse guaranteed to help:

Long-legged Italy kicked little Sicily
Right into the middle of the Mediterranean Sea.

The Streets of Los Angeles

Mnemonics can be used to help you find your way around unfamiliar cities and towns. The following mnemonic mentions 10 primary east to west (actually SE to NW) streets in central LA:

> In LOS ANGELES, you MAINly SPRING
> onto BROADWAY, go up the HILL to OLIVE
> with the GRAND HOPE of picking FLOWERs
> on FIGUEROA.

Grand is actually an avenue not a street, but the idea allows the reader to navigate that part of the city with relative ease by memorizing one simple sentence.

When asked how the Beatles found America on their first U.S. visit:

Just turn left at Greenland....

—John Lennon

5

Animal, Vegetable, Mineral

Geological Periods

The list below details the geological classification of rock deposits, starting with the Cambrian, the first period in the Palaeozoic era.

	Approximate number of years ago
Cambrian	570–510 million
Ordovician	510–439 million
Silurian	439–409 million
Devonian	409–363 million
Carboniferous	363–290 million
Permian	290–245 million
Triassic	245–208 million
Jurassic	208–146 million
Cretaceous	146–65 million
Palaeocene	65–56.5 million
Eocene	56.5–35.4 million
Oligocene	35.4–23.3 million
Miocene	23.3–5.2 million
Pliocene	5.2–1.64 million

Pleistocene   1,640,000–10,000
Recent   (Holocene)   10,000–present day

Large mammals flourished and became extinct as recently as the Pleistocene period, during which time anatomically modern humans most likely began to evolve. The Recent period marked the end of the last Ice Age and the start of the development of modern civilization.

Here's a memorable phrase to help you tell your Eocene from the Pliocene period, starting with the Cambrian era from more than 500 million years ago:

Camels **O**ften **S**it **D**own **C**arefully.
Perhaps **T**heir **J**oints **C**reak? **P**ossibly **E**arly **O**iling
Might **P**revent **P**ermanent **R**heumatism.

Components of Soil

When testing the soil for its age, geologists also need to know the main constituents of soil—namely, **A**ir, **H**umus, **M**ineral salts, **W**ater, **B**acteria and **R**ock particles—which can be remembered with this essential saying:

All **H**airy **M**en **W**ill **B**uy **R**azors.

The Hardness of Minerals

The Mohs Scale, devised in 1822 by German mineralogist Friedrich Mohs (1773–1839), lists 10 familiar, easily available minerals and arranges them in order of their "scratch hardness." Scratch hardness involves a mineral's resistance to fracture or its permanent deformation due to friction from a sharp object.

Minerals in order from softest to hardest:

1. **T**alc
2. **G**ypsum
3. **C**alcite
4. **F**luorite (fluorspar)
5. **A**patite
6. **O**rthoclase (feldspar)
7. **Q**uartz
8. **T**opaz
9. **C**orundum
10. **D**iamond

Groups 1–2 can be scratched by a fingernail.
Groups 3–6 can be scratched with a blade.
Groups 7–10 are hard enough to scratch glass.

A couple of useful mnemonics to memorize the Mohs Scale are:

Tall **G**irls **C**an **F**lirt **A**nd **O**ther **Q**ueer **T**hings **C**an **D**evelop.

TAll **GY**roscopes **CA**n **FL**y **AP**art **OR**biting **QU**ickly **TO** **CO**mplete **DI**sintegration.

Types of Fossils

One way of learning the different types of fossils is to remember the acronym IMAP, which stands for:

Imprint
Moulds (or casts)
Actual remains
Petrified

Or keep in mind the following apt phrase:

I Marvel **At P**etrification.

Stalactites and Stalagmites

Stalactites form when water containing calcium carbonate dissolves after seeping down through limestone or chalk, then evaporates, leaving deposits of carbonates of lime to accumulate over time to form mineral columns in caves. Stalagmites develop in the same way when rain falls onto the floor of caves and minerals build up to form pillars.

The similarity between the spelling and pronunciation of the two words sometimes causes confusion, so several memory aids have been developed to help simplify matters.

The following example relies on the difference in spelling, using the *c* and the *g* to relate to the origin of the formation:

StalaCtites are formed on the Ceiling.

StalaGmites are formed on the Ground.

A slightly sillier way is to think of the reaction to having ants (mites) in your pants:

When mites go up, the tights come down!

A couple of other suggestions have been:

Stalactites hang *tight* from the roof;

Stalagmites *might* reach the roof.

Stalactites hang down like *tight*s on a clothesline;

Stalagmites *might* bite if you sit on them.

Camels: One Lump or Two

There are two main types of camel—one has one hump and the other has two. But what's the best way to remember which is which?

A **B**actrian camel's back is shaped like the letter *b*
—it has two humps.

A **D**romedary's back is shaped like the letter *d*
—it has only one hump.

Both species of camel come from the dry deserts of Asia and North Africa. The Bactrian, or two-humped, camel inhabits central Asia. The Dromedary, or one-humped camel, is a light and fast breed, otherwise known as the Arabian camel. The name comes from the Greek word *dromas*—to run. The Dromedary is domesticated and no longer lives in the wild.

Elephants Never Forget

How do you tell the difference between an Indian (Asian) elephant and an African elephant? It's all in the size, as this rhyme proves:

India's big, and its elephant there features,
But Africa's bigger with much bigger creatures.

Generally the ears of an African elephant are bigger than those of its Indian counterpart. Imagine that those ears resemble the shape of the larger African continent, while those of the Indian elephant are the shape of India.

Insect Stings

From one of the world's largest creatures to two of the smallest. What home remedies will effectively treat a bee or a wasp sting?

Use **A**mmonia for a **B**ee sting

And **V**inegar for a **W**asp sting.

B follows **A** and **W** follows **V**

(Think of the VW car as well).

This is also a useful mnemonic with which to remember the Latin family classification of bees and wasps:

Apidae are **B**ees.

Vespidae are **W**asps.

More correctly, the Apidae classification refers to the "superfamily" of bees, while Vespidae is the "family" classification for wasps.

Taxonomic Classifications

Not to be confused with the art of preparing, stuffing and mounting animal skins (taxidermy), alpha taxonomy is the principle of arranging groups of living organisms—that is, plants and animals—into groups based on similarities of structure and origin. To give an example of the classifications, here are the definitions of man or *homo sapiens:*

Kingdom	*Animalia*
Phylum	*Vertibrata*
Class	*Mammalia*
Order	*Primate*
Family	*Hominidae*
Genus	*Homo*
Species	*Sapiens*
Variety	—

To remember the different classifications including "variety," these two phrases supply strong visual memory aids:

Krakatoa **P**ositively **C**asts **O**ff **F**umes
Generating **S**ulphurous **V**apours.

Kindly **P**lace **C**over **O**n **F**resh **G**reen **S**pring **V**egetables

Versions excluding reference to "variety" can be remembered by using the following phrases:

Kids **P**refer **C**heese **O**ver **F**ried **G**reen **S**pinach.
Kim **P**ut **C**heese **O**n **F**rank's **G**reen **S**hoes.
Kings **P**lay **C**hess **O**n **F**ine **G**reen **S**ilk.

Cedar Trees

Evergreen cedar trees in many parks and gardens come in three types:

Atlas has **A**scending branches.

Lebanon has **L**evel branches.

Deodar has **D**rooping branches.

The Cedar tree has a long history, dating back to biblical times. The Cherokee Amerindians believed that cedar trees held the spirits of ancient ancestors. The Atlas cedar, which grows in southern Canada, makes a popular specimen tree, and is used today in some aromatherapies. Lebanon cedar trees were coveted in ancient times for their appearance, fragrance, and commercial value, particularly in the building industry and today they are a threatened conifer. The massive Deodar cedar tree can reach approximately 250 feet in its original Himalayan habitat. Deodar, from the Sanskrit *devadaru*, translates into "timber of the gods."

Firewood

If you are building a fire at home or making a campfire, consider this traditional poem on the opposite page to avoid suffocating smoke and flying sparks.

Beech wood fires are bright and clear,
If the logs are kept a year.
Chestnut's only good, they say,
If for long it's laid away.
Birch and fir logs burn too fast,
Blaze up bright and do not last.
It is, by the Irish said,
Hawthorn makes the sweetest bread
Elm wood burns like a churchyard mould,
Even the very flames are cold.
Poplar gives a bitter smoke,
Fills your eyes and makes you choke.
Apple wood will scent your room
With an incense-like perfume.
Oak and maple, if dry and old,
Keep away the winter cold.
But ash wood wet and ash wood dry,
A king shall warm his slippers by.

6

Time and the Calendar

Spring Forward, Fall Back

The seasons change, the clocks go back and forth, time waits for no man, and woe betide the person who forgets to reset his or her clock at the beginning of autumn and spring.

Most of North America begins Daylight Saving Time at 2:00 A.M. on the second Sunday in March and reverts to standard time on the first Sunday in November. In Canada, Daylight Saving Time is determined by provincial legislation. Exceptions may be made for certain municipalities. Most of Saskatchewan remains on Central Standard time year round. One of the main goals of daylight saving is to reduce pattterns of energy consumption.

Another advantage to daylight saving time is that many fire

departments urge people to change the batteries in their smoke detectors on the same day that they change their clocks. This provides a convenient reminder.

So in the **spring** the clocks move **forward** one hour to herald summer, and in autumn (or **fall**) they are set **back** one hour to welcome winter.

A similar saying to "Spring Forward, Fall Back" adapted to the new system reminds people of the change in time: "Forward March, back November." That is all you need to remember.

Thirty Days Hath September...

The words to this rhyme are possibly the most often-repeated of all memory aids. This verse, first learned in childhood, helps to recall how many days there are in each month.

The origin of the "Thirty Days Hath September" poem is obscure, but the use of "old" English in the verse suggests that it dates back to at least the sixteenth century. Several different endings to the last two lines of the verse have been recorded, two are listed below:

> Thirty days hath September,
> April, June, and November;
> All the rest have thirty-one
> Excepting February alone,
> And that has twenty-eight days clear,
> With twenty-nine in each leap year.

> Which hath but twenty-eight, in fine,
> Till leap year gives it twenty-nine.

The verse informs the reader that four particular months contain 30 days, and February has either 28 or 29. Therefore, by process of elimination we can work out that the remaining seven months all comprise 31 days. February was the last month in the Julian calendar year; that's the reason it was left to pick up the leftovers.

Days of the Months by Hand

A physical mnemonic trick that can help determine the days of each month is right on the back of your hands. Place your clenched fists together, side by side, and begin with your left hand, naming the knuckle of your little finger as January. The valley or dip between the first two knuckles is February, the knuckle of the ring finger is March, and the next valley is April. July marks the last knuckle on the left hand, and August marks the first knuckle on the right hand, since both months have 31 days. Carry on until you reach the penultimate knuckle on your right hand, representing December. The two thumb knuckles are both excluded from this technique.

All the knuckles represent months with 31 days, and the valleys the shorter months. As in the rhyme, remember that February is the exception. So if you can't remember the famous verse, you can rely on your own hands to jog your memory. A similar memory devise uses the piano keyboard, moving from January, represented by the "F" key, and moving up the keyboard in semitones—the black notes indicate the short months and the white the long months.

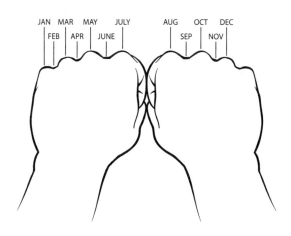

Teaching the Days of the Week

Teaching young children the days of the week poses a challenge for many parents and preschool teachers. The melody to "Clementine" *(Oh, my darlin', oh, my darlin', oh, my darlin', Clementine...)* provides a rhythmic background to the following verse:

> Sunday, Monday,
> Tuesday, Wednesday,
> Thursday, Friday, Saturday,
>
> There are seven days,
> There are seven days,
> There are seven days in a week.

Another musical variation uses the tune to the old TV show *The Addams Family:*

> Days of the week (clap, clap)
> Days of the week (clap, clap)
> There's Sunday and there's Monday
> There's Tuesday and there's Wednesday
> There's Thursday and there's Friday
> And then there's Sat-ur-day.
> Days of the week (clap, clap)
> Days of the week (clap, clap)
> Days of the week, days of the week, days of the week (clap, clap).

Teachers and parents can point to the days on a calendar as the children sing the song, to further help with placement and word identification.

How to Remember Dates

Writer and educator Grace Fleming writes a column on homework and study tips. She claims that an effective way to remember an important date is to think of a silly, visual term that rhymes with the date to imbed the thought into one's consciousness. Here are some examples that use the system:

> You can leave off the century, so that 1867, the year of Confederation, becomes 67.

> Example:
> 67 = Go to heaven

Imagine an airline ticket agent with a halo and angel's wings. It may sound silly, but the technique works!

1885 was the year of the North-West Rebellion, led by Louis Riel, who was apprehended and later hanged. To remember this, you could think:

> 85 = Captured alive

Think of the enigmatic Métis leader being led away in handcuffs to face his dismal fate.

This strategy also works for the husband who can't seem to remember his wedding anniversary or wife's birthday:

> June 10, I married the hen.
> September 15, treat her like a queen.

Time Travel

When travelling long distances throughout the world, it helps to remember EWG and WEL to calculate if you'll be losing or gaining time during a journey:

> **E**ast to **W**est **G**ains and **W**est to **E**ast **L**oses.

The Caribbean Hurricane Season

The people of the Caribbean and the southern United States are only too aware of the risks of hurricanes, as this mnemonic indicates:

June—Too Soon (first month)

July—Stand By (for any news of a storm)

August—You Must (prepare in case a storm comes)

September—Remember (to stand by)

October—It's All Over (last month)

The Signs of the Zodiac

Aries	The Ram	March 21 – April 20
Taurus	The Bull	April 21 – May 20
Gemini	The Twins	May 21 – June 20
Cancer	The Crab	June 21 – July 22
Leo	The Lion	July 23 – August 22
Virgo	The Virgin	August 23 – September 22
Libra	The Scales	September 23 – October 22
Scorpio	The Scorpion	October 23 – November 21
Sagittarius	The Archer	November 22 – December 21
Capricorn	The Goat	December 22 – January 19
Aquarius	The Water Bearer	January 20 – February 18
Pisces	The Fish	February 19 – March 20

The first letters of the words in this mnemonic sentence provide the signs of the astrological zodiac in order, which can be remembered with these phrases:

**All The Great Chancellors Live Very Long
Since Shops Can't Alter Politics.**

A Tense **G**rey **C**at **L**ay **V**ery **L**ow
Sneaking **S**lowly, **C**ontemplating **A P**ounce.

Alternatively, if starting from January, the order changes:
Capricorn, **A**quarius, **P**isces, **A**ries, **T**aurus, **G**emini,
Cancer, **L**eo, **V**irgo, **L**ibra, **S**corpio, **S**agittarius:

Can **A**ll **P**eople **A**lways **T**ake **G**ood **C**are
Lighting **V**aluable **L**amps **S**urrounding **S**askatoon?

To recall the list with a sense of rhythm instead, use the verse written by preacher, poet and hymn writer Isaac Watts (1674–1748), which starts with Aries:

> The *Ram*, the *Bull*, the Heavenly *Twins*,
> And next the *Crab*, the *Lion* shines,
> The *Virgin* and the *Scales*;
> The *Scorpion*, *Archer* and *Sea Goat*.
> The *Man* who held the watering out
> And *Fish* with glittering tails.

Or perhaps try this alternative from E. Cobham Brewer's *Dictionary of Phrase & Fable* (1899):

> Our vernal signs the *Ram* begins
> Then comes the *Bull*, in May the *Twins*;
> The *Crab* in June, next *Leo* shines,
> And *Virgo* ends the northern signs.
> The *Balance* brings autumnal fruits,
> The *Scorpion* stings, the *Archer* shoots;
> December's *Goat* brings wintry blast,
> *Aquarius* rain, the *Fish* come last.

> *The events in our lives happen in a sequence in time, but in their significance to ourselves they find their own order: the continuous thread of revelation.*
>
> —Eudora Welty

7

The Sky at Night and by Day

The Order of the Planets

Before August 2006, the planets of the solar system were **M**ercury, **V**enus, **E**arth, **M**ars, **J**upiter, **S**aturn, **U**ranus, **N**eptune, and **P**luto. Their initial letters lent themselves to all sorts of phrases:

My **V**ery **E**asy **M**ethod: **J**ust **S**et **U**p **N**ine **P**lanets.

My **V**ery **E**ducated **M**other **J**ust **S**erved **U**s **N**ine **P**izzas.

Mom's **V**ery **E**arly **M**orning **J**elly **S**andwiches **U**sually **N**auseate **P**eople.

In August 2006, the International Astronomical Union decided to downgrade the status of Pluto, and so some new mnemonic phrases that don't mention poor old Pluto have been devised for the new generation of stargazers:

My **V**ery **E**ducated **M**other **J**ust **S**erved **U**s **N**achos.

My **V**ery **E**nergetic **M**other **J**ust **S**ent **U**s **N**owhere.

My **V**ery **E**ducated **M**other **J**ust **S**ent **U**s **N**uts.

My **V**ery **E**xotic **M**istress **J**ust **S**erved **U**s **N**oodles.

The four planets closest to the sun are **M**ercury, **V**enus, **E**arth, and **M**ars. These are called the "rocky," or "terrestrial," planets. They are small in relation to other planets, and consist of similar materials to Earth:

My **V**isitor **E**ats **M**ice.

My **V**irgin **E**ats **M**en.

My **V**oice **E**xpects **M**ore.

The "gas" planets are **J**upiter, **S**aturn, **U**ranus, and **N**eptune, which all have rings and moons, and consist mainly of hydrogen, helium, frozen water, ammonia, methane, and carbon monoxide:

Jelly **S**andwiches **U**sually **N**eeded

Joyful **S**usan's **U**nder-**N**ourished

John **S**mith **U**psets **N**eighbours

Saturn's Moons

Saturn has a number of moons. The count is currently 59 with three of them unconfirmed. The fifty-seventh (S/2007 S 1) was discovered on April 13, 2007, and the fifty-eighth and fifty-ninth (S/2007 S 2 and S/2007 S 3) on May 1, 2007.

Saturn moon spottings have increased significantly since the advent of the Voyager missions and the Hubble

Space Telescope; therefore, many books and websites are not accurate or up-to-date. A mnemonic, put into practice prior to the discovery of most of these moons, helped students to memorize the following nine moons of Saturn: Mimas, Enceladus, Tethys, Dione, Rhea, Titan, Hyperion, Iapetus, and Phoebe.

MET DR THIP

The Brightest Stars in the Sky

Positioned at the centre of the solar system, the closest star to Earth is the sun. The brightest stars visible from Earth are listed below, along with the constellation where each is located:

Sir Can Rig A VCR, PA

Sir	Sirius in Canis Major
Can	Canopus in Carina
Rig	Rigil Kent in Centaurus
A	Arcturus in Boötes
V	Vega in Lyra
C	Capella in Auriga
R	Rigel in Orion
P	Procyon in Canis Minor
A	Achernar in Eridanus

The Earth's Atmospheres

Troposphere: extends from the Earth's surface to approximately 6–10 km (3.72–6.21 miles).

Stratosphere: extends to approximately 10–50 km (6.21–31.06 miles) above the Earth.

Mesosphere: located 50–80 km (31.06–49.7 miles) above the Earth's surface.

Thermosphere: located more than 80 km (49.7 miles) above the Earth.

Exosphere: the outermost layer of the atmosphere at 500–1,000 km (310.6–621.37 miles) above the Earth.

To help recall the order of the Earth's atmospheres, the following phrases may act as helpful reminders:

The **S**trong **M**an's **T**riceps **E**xplode.

The **S**traight **M**an's **T**hrottle **E**xcites.

Men on the Moon

Named after the Greek god of the sun, the Apollo program was a series of manned space flights that aimed to land a man on the moon by the end of the 1960s. On

July 20, 1969, Neil Armstrong accomplished this mission when he became the first man to walk on the moon. Armstrong was a member of the crew of Apollo 11, which we can remember by the double *ll* in "Apollo." The names of Armstrong and his fellow astronauts can be recalled with the simple use of ABC:

Neil **A**rmstrong

Buzz Aldrin

Michael **C**ollins

The Apollo program lasted until only 1975, when it was cut short due to rising costs. Only 12 men have ever walked on the moon: Neil Armstrong, Buzz Aldrin, Pete Conrad, Alan Bean, Alan Shepard, Edgar Mitchell, David Scott, James Irwin, John W. Young, Charles Duke, Eugene Cernan, and Harrison Schmitt.

Colours of the Rainbow

When a rainbow appears in the sky as a result of the refraction and dispersion of the sun's rays by light or other water droplets, the seven colours that are said to be visible are: **R**ed, **O**range, **Y**ellow, **G**reen, **B**lue, **I**ndigo, and **V**iolet.

"**R**ichard **O**f **Y**ork **G**ave **B**attle **I**n **V**ain" is the popular mnemonic phrase. It refers to the Battle of Bosworth in 1485, when King Richard III was defeated by Henry Tudor, who became, as Henry VII, the first king of the Tudor dynasty. However, it can also be fun to make up other phrases, such as:

Run **O**ff **Y**ou **G**irls, **B**oys **I**n **V**iew!

Ran **O**ut **Y**esterday, **G**ot **B**ombed **I**n **V**ineyard

Still, other people prefer to recall the colours by making up a man's name: **ROY G BIV**.

Nowadays, however, it is widely believed that indigo does not strictly appear in the spectrum but was merely included by Sir Isaac Newton, the seventeenth-century English physicist and mathematician, because seven colours were considered to be better than six.

Weather Forecasting

A red sky at night; shepherd's delight,
A red sky in the morning; shepherd's warning.

The origins of this rhyme can be traced back to St. Matthew's Gospel in the Bible:

> *When evening comes, you say, "It will be fair weather, for the sky is red," and in the morning, "It will be foul weather today, for the sky is red and overcast."*

Although the words refer to a shepherd who would say that a red sky in the morning would indicate inclement weather to follow, the words could pertain to a sailor's predictions:

Red sky at night, sailor's delight;
Red sky at morning, sailors take warning.

Hundreds of years ago, before any accurate means of weather forecasting became available, people had to rely on those with knowledge and experience, such as sailors and shepherds, whose lives depended on the weather and its changing moods.

Fahrenheit and Celsius

With a few die-hard countries still clinging to the Fahrenheit scale, deciding whether to pack a sweater or a coat can get awfully confusing. Here are two basic formulas to help navigate between the two:

> Fahrenheit to Celsius:
> From F, subtract 32
> Divide that by 9, but before you're through
> Multiply that whole by 5
> To Celsius, you will arrive.
>
> Celsius to Fahrenheit:
> Multiply C by 9
> Divide the answer then by 5
> Next, all you need to do, is to add 32.

8

The World of Science

Chemistry instructors expect their students to have a sound, working knowledge of the names and properties of the 100+ chemical elements of the Periodic Table. It's crucial that students learn not only a chemical's unique properties but also how it reacts with other elements, because getting it wrong can have disastrously flat, fizzy, or fiery consequences.

The Periodic Table of Elements

The Periodic Table was devised in 1869 by Russian chemist Dmitri Mendeleyev. The elements are arranged in increasing order of atomic number from left to right across the table so that elements with similar atomic structures and chemical properties appear in vertical columns. The horizontal rows are called periods, and the vertical rows are known as groups.

Setting a long list of strange names to music is a tried and tested way to remember them. Music has a structure and flow, so if the words fit, they fly off the tongue with ease. Singer-songwriter and mathematician Tom Lehrer concocted his own version of Gilbert and Sullivan's "I Am the Very Model of a Modern Major-General," a song from the comic opera *The Pirates of Penzance*. To hear the ditty sung live, simply type "The element song" into youtube.com.

There's antimony, arsenic, aluminum, selenium,
And hydrogen and oxygen and nitrogen and rhenium,
And nickel, neodymium, neptunium, germanium,
And iron, americium, ruthenium, uranium,
Europium, zirconium, lutetium, vanadium,
And lanthanum and osmium and astatine and radium,
And gold and protactinium and indium and gallium,

[Gasp]

And iodine and thorium and thulium and thallium.
There's yttrium, ytterbium, actinium, rubidium,
And boron, gadolinium, niobium, iridium,
And strontium and silicon and silver and samarium,
And bismuth, bromine, lithium, beryllium and barium.
There's holmium and helium and hafnium and erbium,
And phosphorus and francium and fluorine and terbium,

And manganese and mercury, molybdenum, magnesium,

Dysprosium and scandium and cerium and caesium.

And lead, praseodymium, and platinum, plutonium,

Palladium, promethium, potassium, polonium,

And tantalum, technetium, titanium, tellurium,

[Pause for deep breath]

And cadmium and calcium and chromium and curium.

There's sulfur, californium, and fermium, berkelium,

And also mendelevium, einsteinium, nobelium,

And argon, krypton, neon, radon, xenon, zinc and rhodium,

And chlorine, carbon, cobalt, copper, tungsten, tin and sodium.

These are the only ones of which the news has come to Harvard,

And there may be many others, but they haven't been discavard!

In addition to the 102 elements listed above, there are a few more that complete the list; namely, lawrencium, rutherfordium, dubnium, seaborgium, bohrium, hassium, meitnerium, darmstadtium, iroentgenium, and seven others, which have yet to be named.

Here are some ways of remembering the first 18 elements in the periodic table, which occupy the first three periods:

Periods 1–2 (Elements 1–10)

H	Hydrogen
He	Helium
Li	Lithium
Be	Beryllium
B	Boron
C	Carbon
N	Nitrogen
O	Oxygen
F	Fluorine
Ne	Neon

Happy **H**enry **L**ikes **B**aking **B**ig **C**akes,
Not **O**mitting **F**loury **N**uggets.

Happy **H**enry **L**ikes **B**eer
But **C**ould **N**ot **O**btain **F**our **N**uts.

Period 3 (Elements 11–18)

Na	Sodium
Mg	Magnesium
Al	Aluminum
Si	Silicon
P	Phosphorus

S	Sulfur
Cl	Chlorine
Ar	Argon

Naughty **M**agpies **A**lways **S**ing **P**erfect **S**ongs **C**lawing **A**nts.

The Most Common Magnetic Material

The four most common magnetic materials are **N**ickel, **I**ron, **C**obalt, and **S**teel, which can be remembered by the clever saying:

Nick **I**rons **C**reased **S**hirts.

Oxidation and Reduction

Oxidation is the loss of an electron by a molecule, an atom, or an ion. Reduction is the opposite; that is, the gain of an electron by molecule, atom, or ion. A simple example of an oxidation—reduction reaction (you can't have one without the other) is the reaction of hydrogen gas with oxygen gas to form water: $2H_2 + O_2 = 2H_2O$.

Many students have found the OILRIG acronym an invaluable method of understanding the process:

Oxidation **Is** **L**oss (of electrons)

Reduction **Is** **G**ain (of electrons)

Parts of an Atom

PEN is possibly the simplest acronym in the history of mnemonics:

Proton, **E**lectron, **N**eutron

CFCs

CFCs have invaded the language and the atmosphere. Thomas Midgley, an organic chemist at General Motors Corporation, discovered chlorofluorocarbons (CFCs) in the 1920s. They are a group of gases believed to contribute to global warming by eroding the ozone layer. The gases that come from leaking air conditioners, refrigerators, and aerosols take 10 to 20 years to reach the stratosphere and remain there for 65 years.

Because the word chlorofluorocarbons doesn't exactly roll off the tongue, some thoughtful soul shortened the word to **CFC**, to keep this vital word in the forefront of our minds.

The Speed of Light

In the same way that it is possible to remember pi to different numbers of decimal places, a simple phrase also enables us to recall the speed of light in metres per second:

We guarantee certainty, clearly referring to this light mnemonic = 299,792,458 m/sec.

Chemistry Experiments: A Warning

And here's a warning to all would-be chemists about the dangers of confusing water with sulfuric acid:

Johnny was a chemist,
But Johnny is no more,
For what he thought was H_2O,
Was H_2SO_4!

The capacity to blunder slightly is the real marvel of DNA. Without this special attribute, we would still be anaerobic bacteria, and there would be no music.

—Lewis Thomas

9
World History

The Greek Philosophers

The names of the three most important Greek philosophers, in order of their dates of birth and also their influence, are:

        Socrates (469–399 BC)
        Plato (c. 429–c. 347 BC)
        Aristotle (384–322 BC)

Socrates taught Plato, and Plato taught Aristotle. Together they created the foundations of Western philosophy. Use your visual memory and imagine them meditating in a health **SPA**. Or think of the phrase: **S**mart **P**eople of **A**thens.

Roman Emperors

After Julius Caesar, the Roman general and statesman who became dictator of the Roman Empire before his assassination in 44 BC, the first five emperors of Rome were all Caesars. The first emperor was Julius Caesar's adopted son (and great-nephew), Augustus, who handed down the title to his son-in-law Tiberius. From Augustus to Nero, Caesar's descendants, by adoption, marriage, or birth, all inherited the family name:

Augustus	(31 BC–AD 14)
Tiberius	(AD 14–37)
Caligula	(AD 37–41)
Claudius	(AD 41–54)
Nero	(AD 54–68)

Here's a phrase to help remember the names by which they were most commonly known:

Another **T**om **C**at **C**aught **N**apping.

The next six Roman emperors after Nero are **G**alba, **O**tho, **V**itellius, **V**espasian, **T**itus, **D**omitian:

At **T**he **C**at **C**lub **N**ever **G**ive **O**ut
Violent **V**ermin **T**o **D**ogs

The Seven Wonders of the Ancient World

The seven wonders of the ancient world were chronicled in the second century B.C.; a list has also been discovered in *The Histories of Herodotus* from the fifth century B.C. The final list of amazing monuments to religion, mythology, and art was compiled in the Middle Ages.

1. **S**tatue of Zeus at Olympia
2. **L**ighthouse (Pharos) of Alexandria
3. **M**ausoleum of Halicarnassus
4. **P**yramids of Egypt
5. **H**anging Gardens of Babylon
6. **T**emple of Artemis at Ephesus
7. **C**olossus of Rhodes

This mnemonic phrase has proved useful in remembering the seven wonders:

Seems **L**ike **M**ata **H**ari **P**icked **H**er **T**argets **C**arefully.

Mythological Matters

Mnemosyne is the Greek goddess of memory, daughter of Gaia and Uranus. She lay with Zeus for nine nights and gave birth to the nine Muses: **C**alliope, **E**uterpe, **C**lio, **E**rato, **M**elpomene, **P**olyhymnia, **T**erpsichore, **T**halia, and **U**rania.

Carol **E**ats **C**runchy **E**ggs,
Mashed **P**otatoes, **T**hen **T**hrows **U**p.

Clarrissa **E**ats **C**andy **E**very **M**orning,
Politely **T**aking **T**urns.

In classical art, the Muses are represented by emblems, or mnemonic symbols, of which the masks of comedy and tragedy are probably the most familiar.

Name	Association	Mnemonic symbol
Calliope	Chief of the muses and muse of epic poetry	writing tablet
Euterpe	Muse of music	flute
Clio	Muse of history	scroll and books
Erato	Muse of love poetry	lyre and crown of roses
Melpomene	Muse of tragedy	tragic mask
Polyhymnia	Muse of sacred poetry	pensive expression

Terpsichore	Muse of dance	dancing with a lyre
Thalia	Muse of comedy	comic mask
Urania	Muse of astronomy	staff and celestial globe

Joan of Arc

Also known as the Maid of Orléans, French national heroine Joan of Arc (c. 1412–1431) claimed that it was God's mission for her to reclaim her homeland from English domination toward the end of the Hundred Years War. She triumphed at the Siege of Orléans in 1429, which led to Charles VII's coronation at Reims, but was later captured at a skirmish near Compiègne. The English regent John of Lancaster, first Duke of Bedford, had her burned at the stake at Rouen when she was only 19. She was canonized in 1920.

This mnemonic phrase describes the short life of Joan of Arc:

ORLEANS CAMPAIGN RUIN

Orleans – victory – 1429

Compiègne – capture – 1430

Rouen – trial and death – 1431

The Six Wives of Henry VIII

Henry VIII (1491–1547) married six times in a quest to have a son and heir. His decision to divorce his first wife and remarry was the root of the split of the Roman Catholic Church, the dissolution of the monasteries, and the formation of the Church of England. The following is a list of Henry's wives in order of marriage dates from first to last:

>1510—Catherine of Aragon (mother of Mary I)
>1533—Anne Boleyn (mother of Elizabeth I)
>1536—Jane Seymour (mother of Edward VI)
>1540—Anne of Cleves
>1540—Catherine Howard
>1543—Catherine Parr

Use this rhythmic couplet to remember their first names:

>Kate & Anne & Jane & Anne & Kate again & again!

Using the initial letters of their surnames gives the phrase:

>**A**ll **B**oys **S**hould **C**ome **H**ome, **P**lease.

The following memorable rhyme reveals the ultimate fate of these six women:

> Divorced, beheaded, died,
> Divorced, beheaded, survived.

Brief History of the United States

The following verse was devised by American poet and former child prodigy Winifred Sackville Stoner, Jr. (1902–1983). She was best known for writing mnemonic rhymes and poems to help people recall important information, particularly for educational purposes. One of her most famous poems is "The History of the U.S." The poem contains 19 stanzas, but people often remember only the first one or two. It paints an often-unrealistic picture of U.S. history but serves as a clever mnemonic to remember those important historical dates. Below you will find the first five stanzas, which start in 1492, along with the final stanza, which brings the reader all the way to 1918 and the end of WWI.

> In fourteen hundred ninety-two,
> Columbus sailed the ocean blue

And found this land, land of the Free,
beloved by you, beloved by me.

And in the year sixteen and seven,
good Captain Smith thought he'd reach Heav'n,
And then he founded Jamestown City,
alas, 'tis gone, oh, what a pity.

'Twas in September sixteen nine,
with ship, Half Moon, a read Dutch sign,
That Henry Hudson found the stream,
the Hudson River of our dream.

In sixteen twenty, pilgrims saw
our land that had no unjust law.
Their children live here to this day
proud citizens of U.S.A.

In sixteen hundred eighty-three,
good William Penn stood 'neath a tree
And swore that unto his life's end
he would be the Indian's friend.

…Thank God in nineteen eighteen,
Peace on earth again was seen,
And we are praying that she'll stay
forever in our U.S.A.

The Pilgrim Fathers

In 1620 a group of English puritans who had fled to Holland to avoid religious persecution returned to England and sailed on the *Mayflower* from Plymouth to the New World. After a long, treacherous journey, they landed at Cape Cod, Massachusetts.

Nothing abbreviates this voyage more cleverly than the *Schoolhouse Rock* cartoon from the 1970s, "No More Kings."

> The pilgrims sailed the sea
> To find a place to call their own.
> In their ship, *Mayflower*,
> They hoped to find a better home.
> They finally knocked
> On Plymouth Rock
> And someone said, "We're there."
> It may not look like home
> But at this point I don't care.

The *Schoolhouse Rock* (SHR) revolution began in 1971, when David McCall, chairman of the ad agency McCaffrey & McCall, noticed that his son could sing all the Beatles and Rolling Stones lyrics but couldn't handle simple math. His solution was to link math with contemporary music. Grammar and history were added to the SHR mix, and the fact that many adults can still sing its phrases today solidly establishes video, combined with song, as an effective mnemonic device.

Declaration of Independence

The date 1776 marks the signing of the U.S. Declaration of Independence. The number of letters in each word in the following sentence stands for a numeral in the date:

I sighted Thomas's rights.

American poet Winifred Sackville Stoner, Jr.'s take on how to remember the date of the Declaration of Independence goes like this:

> Year seventeen hundred seventy-six,
> July the fourth, this date please fix
> Within your minds, my children dear,
> for that was Independence Year.

The Civil War

And regarding the dark days of the American Civil War,
Winifred Sackville Stoner, Jr. wrote:

> In eighteen hundred and sixty-one,
> an awful war was then begun
> Between the brothers of our land,
> who now together firmly stand.

Author and certified holistic counselor Laurel Ann
Browne offers the following civil war mnemonic on her
parenting website:

> Four Bulls Ate Everything Vicky Grew.

It translates into chronological order the major events of
the Civil War.

> **Four**: Fort Sumter, the first shots in the Civil War
> **Bulls**: Battle of Bull Run (First Manassas), the
> first major battle of the Civil War
> **Ate**: Antietam, the bloodiest battle in Civil War
> history with over 20,000 casualties
> **Everything**: Emancipation Proclamation, in
> which Lincoln abolished slavery

Vicky: The battle of Vicksburg, which controlled the Mississippi River for the North
Grew: The Gettysburg Address, four score and seven years ago…

Presidents of the U.S.

To date, 44 U.S. presidents have assumed office, which would make an incredibly long and complicated mnemonic phrase. But the presidents of the twentieth century are:

> **T**heodore Roosevelt (1901–1909)
> William H. **T**aft (1909–1913)
> Woodrow **W**ilson (1913–1921)
> Warren **H**arding (1921–1923)
> Calvin **C**oolidge (1923–1929)
> Herbert **H**oover (1929–1933)
> Franklin D. Roosevelt (1933–1945)
> Harry S **T**ruman (1945–1953)
> Dwight D. **E**isenhower (1953–1961)
> John F. **K**ennedy (1961–1963)
> Lyndon B. **J**ohnson (1963–1969)
> Richard M. **N**ixon (1969–1974)
> Gerald **F**ord (1974–1977)

Jimmy **C**arter (1977–1981)
Ronald **R**eagan (1981–1989)
George H. W. **B**ush (1989–1993)
William J. **C**linton (1992–2001)

Though it's quite a lengthy list, this saying might just make life easier:

Theodore **T**akes **W**ilson's **H**and,
Cool **H**oovering **F**ranklin's **T**rue **E**xperiences.
Ken, **J**ustly **N**oted **F**or **C**andor, **R**uled **B**ut **C**oolly.

The Heads on Mount Rushmore

Mount Rushmore is a famous national memorial in South Dakota, which represents the first 150 years of U.S. history with 18-metre (60-foot) high granite carvings of the heads of four great U.S. presidents: **W**ashington, **J**efferson, Lincoln, and **R**oosevelt.

We **J**ust **L**ike **R**ushmore.

Prime Ministers of Canada

To date, 22 Canadian prime ministers have been sworn in, which would make a long and complicated mnemonic phrase. The names of the first 11 prime ministers are:

John A. Macdonald (1867–1873, 1878–1891)
Alexander MacKenzie (1873–1878)
John Abbott (1891–1892)
John Thompson (1892–1894)
Mackenzie Bowell (1894–1896)
Charles Tupper (1896)
Wilfrid Laurier (1896–1911)
Robert L. Borden (1911–1920)
Arthur Meighen (1920–1921, 1926)
William Lyon Mackenzie King (1921–1926,
1926–1930, 1935–1948)
Richard B. Bennett (1930–1935)

Here's a question to ponder to help recall the first 11:

Mac's Macaw Appreciates Tea Biscuits. Those Little Biscuits Make Kangaroos Bounce.

And here are the remaining Canadian prime ministers who have served until present:

Louis Saint-Laurent (1948–1957)
John Diefenbaker (1957–1963)
Lester B. Pearson (1963–1968)
Pierre Elliott Trudeau (1969–1979, 1980–1984)
Joseph "Joe" Clark (1979–1980)
John Turner (1984)
Brian Mulroney (1984–1993)
Kim Campbell (1993)
Jean Chrétien (1993–2003)
Paul Martin (2003–2006)
Stephen Harper (2006)

To recall this eminent list of 14, keep in mind the following phrase:

Seven **D**angerous **P**irates **T**ake **C**harge, **T**elling **M**ischievous **C**annibals, "**C**reate **M**ass **H**ysteria!"

World War I (The Great War)

Once called the War to End All Wars, this massive military conflict took 20 million lives. Many factors contributed to the outbreak of this global war. The word

ANIMAL assists people in remembering some of the most prominent causes.

> **A**ssassination—Archduke Franz Ferdinand of Austria-Hungary and his wife were assassinated on June 28, 1914.

> **N**ationalism—This time period saw a rise in strong patriotic sentiments and loyalty toward home countries.

> **I**mperialism—Colonization was common at the turn of the century, and countries competed for territory and economic advantage.

> **M**ilitarism—France, Britain and Germany had well-established military might, and an arms race ensued.

> **AL**liance System—War with any allied nation meant war with the whole alliance. This system was meant to discourage aggression but failed.

We learn from history that we learn nothing from history.

—George Bernard Shaw

10

Musical Interlude

Music can be a mnemonic device all by itself: advertisers often use musical jingles to get their products into our heads. For example, just ten simple notes composed by Steve Karmen in 1970, give us "When you say Budweiser, you've said it all." Karmen is also notorious for the New York State song "I Love New York." And when U.S. Senator Hillary Clinton first launched her campaign for the White House, she adopted "You and I" – an Air Canada jingle – as her official campaign song.

Musical Notes

The first seven letters of the alphabet (A, B, C, D, E, F, G) are used in musical notation, which at least helps to keep it simple. In the 1965 film *The Sound of Music*, Julie Andrews's character Maria makes the learning of music seem so easy.

Do–Re–Mi–Fa–So–La–Ti

Do = doe – a female deer
Re = ray – a drop of golden sun
Mi = me – a name I call myself

Fa = far – a long, long way to run
So = sew – a needle pulling thread
La = la – a note to follow "so"
Ti = tea – a drink with jam and bread
Which will bring us back to "Do"

Musical Staves

Learning to read music notation is almost impossible without the use of mnemonic tools. The musical staff is the set of five lines and four spaces on which notes indicate pitch and rhythm. The treble staff (or clef), indicating higher notes, is generally played with the right hand on the piano, and the bass staff (or clef), indicating lower notes, with the left hand.

Treble Clef: Lines

The notes on the lines of the treble clef are, from the lowest, E, G, B, D, F. They can be remembered with the following common:

Every Good Boy Deserves Fudge

Favor may be replaced by fruit, fudge, or fun, depending on your taste.

Other variations include:

Every **G**ood **B**oy **D**oes **F**ine.

Every **G**irl **B**uys **D**esigner **F**ashions.

Every **G**ood **B**ird **D**oes **F**ly.

Treble Clef: Spaces

The notes on the spaces on the treble clef are, from the lowest, F, A, C, E. This short rhyme may help with learning the order of notes:

If the note's in a space, together they spell FACE.

Bass Clef: Lines

The order of notes on the lines of the bass clef are G, B, D, F, A. "Good boys" return again in the catchy phrase devised to help musicians remember these basics:

Good **B**oys **D**eserve **F**ruit **A**lways.

"Fruit" can, of course, be substituted for another more suitable f-word if necessary.

Other variations include:

Good Boys Don't Fool Around.

Great Big Dogs Fight Always.

Good Bikes Don't Fall Apart.

Great Big Ducks Fly Away.

Gentle Brown Donkeys Favour Apples.

Bass Clef: Spaces

And thus it follows that the notes in the spaces of the bass clef are A, C, E, G. The following sayings act as a useful reminder of the four-note order:

All Cows Eat Grass.

All Cars Eat Gas.

All Cats Eat Goldfish.

The Circle of Fifths

Music theory is not rocket science. There are 12 notes in Western music in one octave, and all you need to do is add, subtract, multiply, and divide. The notes—B, C, C#, D, D#, E, F, F#, G, G#, A, A#—are all half a tone apart.

Major chords are comprised of the root note and the higher third and fifth notes, plus the options of the seventh or eighth. Minor chords are made up of the root note and the minor third and fifth notes of the scale, with the option of the other notes. The circle of fifths is based on taking the fifth note as the root for the next chord. For example, in an F chord the fifth note is C; therefore, the next chord is C, then G and so on—F, C, G, D, A, E, B:

Father **C**harles **G**oes **D**own **A**nd **E**nds **B**attle.

Other variations include:

Father **C**hristmas **G**ets **D**runk **A**fter **E**very **B**eer.

Fat **C**ats **G**o **D**eaf **A**fter **E**ating **B**ats.

Five **C**ool **G**uys **D**anced **A**way **E**very **B**eat.

And in reverse for the flat keys, the mnemonic can be reversed—B♭, E♭, A♭, D♭, G♭, C♭, F♭:

Battle Ends And Down Goes Charles's Father.

Bottles Empty And Down Goes Charles's Father.

Be Exciting And Daring, Go Climb Fences.

Choral Voices

There are four different voice ranges that one can hear in a quartet, whose initial letters helpfully spell out STAB:

Soprano
Tenor
Alto
Bass

Musical Modes or Scales

The modes as based on the white piano keys beginning at C are:

Ionian mode—the familiar major scale in which most popular music is written.

Dorian mode—most often heard in Celtic music, with a melancholy feel.

Phrygian mode—used especially by guitar soloists in counterpoint to an Ionian mode.

Lydian mode—popular in jazz music, with a mix of major and minor chord progressions.

Mixolydian mode—major feel with minor intervals and popular with soloists as a counterpoint to an Ionian mode.

Aeolian mode—in a minor key and produces a sense of sadness.

Locrian mode—the intervals are considered unsatisfactory and most composers find it unworkable.

Named after Greek cities that are thought to reflect the moods of the seven modes, one way of remembering the order of the modes is to recall this phrase:

I Don't **P**lay **L**ike **M**y **A**unt **L**ucy.

11

Other Languages

French Plurals with an X

Here's a verse to tell you which French nouns require the
letter *x* rather than *s* when they are used in the plural:

> *Bijou, caillou, chou,*
> *Genou, hibou, joujou . . .*
> *Pou!*

The English translation of the verse is:

> Jewel, pebble, cabbage,
> Knee, owl, toy . . .
> Flea!

Or commit this rhyme to memory:

> *Mes choux, mes bijoux,*
> *Lassez-vous joujoux,*
> *Venez sur mes genoux!*
> *Regardez ces mauvais petits garçons,*
> *Qui jettent des cailloux a ces pauvres hiboux!*

> My cabbages, my jewels,
> Stop playing with your toys, and come sit on
> my knees!
> Look at these bad little boys,
> Who throw stones at these poor owls!

Counting to Six in French

The correct words for one to six in French are *un, deux, trois, quatre, cinq,* and *six.* Try to picture the horror of this dark story of how to control the cat population:

Un, deux, trois, cat sank—cease, please!

French Verbs Using *Être*

All French verbs that use *être* in the perfect tense rather than *avoir* indicate a particular kind of movement. The

13 main verbs (and four derivatives) can be recalled using the popular mnemonic phrase **Dr. & Mrs. P. Vandertramp**:

Devenir **R**evenir & **M**onter **R**ester **S**ortir
Passer **V**enir **A**ller **N**aître **D**escendre **E**ntrer
Rentrer **T**omber **R**etourner **A**rriver
Mourir **P**artir

Alternatively, the acronym ADVENT is another useful way to recall the main *être* verbs. Each letter stands for one of the verbs and its opposite, with the thirteenth verb— *retourner*—standing alone.

Arriver—Partir
Descendre—Monter
Venir—Aller
Entrer—Sortir
Naître—Mourir
Tomber—Rester
Retourner

Japanese Vowels

The pronunciation and lexical ordering of the Japanese vowels is AIUEO. Using this short phrase, you can understand the pronunciation of the vowels:

Ah, we soon get old.

Counting to 10 in Japanese

Numeral	Japanese word	Sounds like
1	Ichi	Itchy
2	Ni	Knee
3	San	Sun
4	Shi	She
5	Go	Go
6	Roko	Rocko
7	Shichi	Shi Shi
8	Hachi	Hatchy
9	Kyu	Queue
10	Ju	Jew

Days of the Week in French, Spanish, and Italian

The seven-day week has been the norm for almost 2,000 years. The Romans allocated one of the seven planets to each of the days of the week: the sun, moon and the five planets that shine brightly in the night sky—Mars, Mercury, Jupiter, Venus, and Saturn.

	Planet	French	Spanish	Italian
Sunday	Sun	Dimanche	Domingo	Domenica
Monday	Moon	Lundi	Lunes	Lunedì
Tuesday	Mars	Mardi	Martes	Martedì

	Planet	French	Spanish	Italian
Wednesday	Mercury	Mercredi	Miércoles	Mercoledì
Thursday	Jupiter	Jeudi	Jueves	Giovedì
Friday	Venus	Vendredi	Viernes	Venerdì
Saturday	Saturn	Samedi	Sábado	Sabato

By recalling the planets after which the days were named, it helps to jog the memory when remembering the days of the week in the Latin-based languages.

Since many of the planets were named after the gods, this traditional rhyme borrows some of the characteristics of the planets or gods and pairs them with the corresponding days of the week:

> Monday's child is fair of face,
> Tuesday's child is full of grace,
> Wednesday's child is full of woe,
> Thursday's child has far to go;
> Friday's child is loving and giving,
> Saturday's child works hard for a living,
> But the child that is born on the Sabbath day
> Is bonny and blithe, good and gay.

The Greek Alphabet

To learn the Greek alphabet, you can memorize the order of the 24 letters by singing along to the tune of "Twinkle, Twinkle, Little Star," but if you're no longer a child, it might be better not to practice out loud . . .

> Alpha, Beta, Gamma, Delta,
> Epsilon, Zeta, Eta, Theta,
> Iota, Kappa, Lambda, Mu,
> Nu, Xi, Omicron, Pi,
> Rho, Sigma, Tau, Upsilon,
> Phi, Chi, Psi kai Omega.

NB: *K* (kai) means "and" in Greek.

The Runic Alphabet

The Runic alphabet is also known as FUTHARK, after the first six letters in this alphabet—namely *f, u, th, a, r,* and *k.* Variants used by early Scandinavians and Anglo-Saxons had between 16 and 33 letters, but the widest-known system had 24 runes, comprised of 18 consonants and six vowels..

The Runic characters comprise a series of glyphs that represent sounds and ideas, much like the hieroglyphs of Ancient Egypt. They were not only used to convey sacred meaning but also mysteries and secrets. It is not known why the letters were ordered in this way, but the word *Futhark* is considered an ancient mnemonic.

12
Religious Matters

For Christians, most religious instruction comes from Sunday school or religious-education classes. While children listen to countless Bible stories, rhymes and sayings help to simplify certain matters of religion, keeping the vast subjects of the Old Testament and New Testament clear in their minds.

The Twelve Apostles

The twelve chief followers of Jesus are recalled in a well-known Sunday school rhyme:

> This is the way the disciples run
> Peter, Andrew, James, and John
> Philip and Bartholomew
> Thomas next and Matthew, too.
> James the less and Judas the greater
> Simon the zealot and Judas the traitor.

An alternative shorter method uses the following line:

Bart And John Fill (Phil) Tom's Matt with 2 Jameses,
2 Simons,* and 2 Judases.

*Peter was originally Simon or Simon-Peter,
therefore there are two Simons in the second verse.

The Four Gospels

With regard to the first four books of the New Testament (the Gospels), religious leaders and Sunday school teachers have various rhymes to help children remember the names (and their order) more easily.

> Matthew, Mark, Luke, and John
> Went to bed with their trousers on.

The verse is probably derived from the following traditional poem, of which there are two versions:

>Matthew, Mark, Luke, and John
>Bless the bed that I lie on;
>Before I lay me down to sleep,
>I give my soul to Christ to keep.

>Matthew, Mark, Luke, and John
>Bless the bed that I lie on;
>Four corners to my bed,
>Four angels round my head;
>One to watch, one to pray,
>And two to bear my soul away!

The Ten Commandments

The Ten Commandments are a list of rules for living an honest and moral life. According to the Old Testament, they are the word of God, inscribed on two stone tablets and given to Moses on Mount Sinai. James Muirden, author of *The Rhyming Bible*, has cleverly compiled them into an unforgettable verse comprising six rhyming couplets:

>The First Law set by God in stone
>reads *Worship me, and me alone!*
>The next says Idols are profane;
>the Third, don't take my Name in vain;

the Fourth says keep the Seventh Day free;
the Fifth, treat Parents properly;
the Sixth says Murdering is wrong
(you knew the Seventh all along*);
the Eighth is crystal clear on Thieving,
as is the Ninth, on Not Deceiving;
and now the last of all His laws—
don't Covet things that are not yours.

*The Seventh, of course, forbids adultery.

Another way of remembering the commandments is the following:

One idle damn Sunday, Dad killed cheating thief
and lied to cover it.

That is, one God; no idols; don't swear; keep the Sabbath; honor your father (and mother); don't kill; don't commit adultery; don't steal; don't bear false witness; and don't covet.

Books of the Old Testament

Although there are a total of 39 books in the Old Testament (King James Bible), this memorable verse has made it much easier to remember them all in order:

That great Jehovah speaks to us,
In Genesis and Exodus,

Leviticus and Numbers see,
Followed by Deuteronomy,
Joshua and Judges sway the land,
Ruth gleans a sheaf with trembling hand;
Samuel and numerous Kings appear,
Whose Chronicles we wondering hear.
Ezra and Nehemiah now,
Esther, the beauteous mourner show.
Job speaks in sighs, David in Psalms,
The Proverbs teach to scatter alms.
Ecclesiastes then come on,
And the sweet Song of Solomon.
Isaiah, Jeremiah then,
With Lamentations takes his pen,
Ezekiel, Daniel, Hosea's lyres,
Swell Joel, Amos, Obadiah's.
Next Jonah, Micah, Nahum come,
And lofty Habakkuk finds room.
While Zephaniah, Haggai calls,
Rapt Zechariah builds his walls,
And Malachi, with garments rent,
Concludes the Ancient Testament.

The 10 Biblical Plagues of Egypt

From Exodus 7:14–12:36, these are the 10 catastrophes that God inflicted upon Egypt:

River to blood

Frogs

Lice

Flies

Murrain (disease)

Boils

Hail

Locusts

Darkness

Firstborn

If the list proves too tricky to remember, the following sentence is a memorable means of recalling the order and initial letter of each plague:

Robert **F**rost **L**ikes **F**udge **M**ilk
Brownies **H**aving **L**ot of **D**ouble **F**udge

or

Flow **L**ike **F**resh **M**ilk
Behind **H**arry **L**ong's **D**eer **F**ence

The Seven Deadly Sins

There are seven days of the week, seven colours in the rainbow, seven wonders of the world, and for those who have not taken their Bible studies to heart, there are seven deadly sins:

Anger, **P**ride, **C**ovetousness, **L**ust, **S**loth, **E**nvy, **G**reed

To help make the list of sins easier to memorize, some God-fearing person devised the following mnemonic phrase:

All **P**rivate **C**olleges **L**eave **S**erious **E**ducational **G**aps.

Or to put it another way:

Pride, **E**nvy, **W**rath, **S**loth, **A**varice, **G**luttony, **L**ust
PEWS 'Ave GLu

The 10 States of Mind

In the Buddhist construct there are 10 states of mind:

1. **H**ell, the state of suffering
2. **H**unger, the state of base needs
3. **A**nimalism, the state of beastly power
4. **A**nger, the state of loathing
5. **N**eutrality, the state of neither one thing or another
6. **R**apture, the state of joy
7. **L**earning, the state of being mentally open
8. **R**ealization, the state of receiving/living wisdom
9. **B**odhisattva, the state of compassion
10. **B**uddha, the state of perfection

All of that mental agony and ecstasy gives us:

Has Hannah Arranged All Novices Running Late, Required Before Buddha?

13
The Human Body

Young medics often face masses of dull and lengthy lists of complicated words, which represent the workings of the human body. Without a wide range of useful and often-amusing memory aids, it would be impossible for them to remember everything.

The Vital Processes of Life

Collectively, these are known as **MRS. GREN**:

Movement, **R**espiration, **S**ensitivity,
Growth, **R**eproduction, **E**xcretion, **N**utrition

The Human Brain

The brain is the complex structure at the nub of all human decisions, communications, and activities. The cerebral cortex is divided into four sections, or lobes:

Frontal, **P**arietal, **O**ccipital, **T**emporal

First **P**lace **O**ften **T**rounces.

Cranial Bones

Occipital, Parietal, Frontal, Temporal,
Ethmoid, Sphenoid

Old People From Texas Eat Spiders

Cranial Nerves

How many medical students learned the 12 cranial nerves
sung to the tune of "The Twelve Days of Christmas?"
   The first and second verses start off:

I (Olfactory)
On the first nerve of the cranium,
my true love gave to me:
My sense olfactory.

II (Optic)
On the second nerve of the cranium,
my true love gave to me:
Two eyes a-looking,
And my sense olfactory.

The song gets quite lengthy, so the final verse is:

XII (Hypoglossal)
On the twelfth nerve of the cranium,
my true love gave to me:
Twelve lovely lickings, (Hypoglossal)
Eleven heads a-tilting, (Spinal accessory)

Ten heartbeats a minute, (Vagus)
Nine quick swallows, (Glossopharyngeal)
Eight sounds, and balance, (Auditory)
Seven funny faces, (Facial)
Six sideways glances, (Abducens)
Mas-ti-ca-tion! (Trigeminal)
Four superior oblique muscles, (Trochlear)
Three cross-eyed glances, (Oculomotor)
Two eyes a-looking, (Optic)
And my sense olfactory. (Olfactory)

In addition to the song, there is also a catchy phrase to recall when remembering the names of the cranial nerves:

On **O**ld **O**lympus's **T**owering **T**op,
A **F**at-**A**ssed **G**erman **V**iewed **S**ome **H**ops.

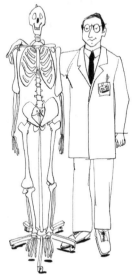

Bones of the Human Body

BONES OF THE UPPER LIMB OR ARM:
Scapula, Clavicle, Humerus, Ulna, Radius, Carpals,
Metacarpals, Phalanges

Some Crooks Have Underestimated Royal Canadian
Mounted Police.

BONES OF THE LOWER LIMB OR LEG:
Hip, Femur, Patella, Tibia, Fibula, Tarsals,
Metatarsals, Phalanges

Help Five Police To Find Ten Missing Prisoners.

BONES OF THE WRIST (CARPAL):
Scaphoid, Lunate, Triquetrum, Pisiform, Trapezium,
Trapezoid, Capitate, Hamate

Some Lovers Try Positions That They Can't Handle.

VERTEBRAE OR BONES OF THE SPINAL COLUMN
(SUPERIOR TO INFERIOR):
Cervical, Dorsal,* Lumbar, Sacrum, Coccyx

Canned Tuna Looks So Cramped.

* Dorsal vertebrae are also known as Thoracic—
therefore, the alternative phrase.

SHOULDER MUSCLES OR ROTATOR CUFF
Teres minor, Infraspinatus, Supraspinatus, Subscapular

Time Is Standing Still.

Bone Fracture Types

Once medical students learn the specific bones, they can use the **GO C3PO** acronym to learn the ways in which the bones can get broken.

Greenstick, Open, Complete/Closed/Comminuted,
Partial, Others

Skin Layers

Mnemonic sentences help medics to remember the order of skin layers or nerves so that when they become surgeons and start brandishing scalpels, they can identify which bit to cut through first. They use the aptly named **SCALP** acronym:

Skin, Connective tissue, Aponeurosis,
Loose areolar tissue, Periosteum

Excretion

For the excretory organs of the body, think **SKILL**:

Skin, Kidneys, Intestines, Liver, Lungs

The Properties of Bile

Here's a catchy ditty to keep the properties of bile in mind:

Bile from the liver emulsifies greases
Tinges the urine and colours the feces
Aids peristalsis, prevents putrefaction
If you remember all this, you'll give satisfaction.

Doctors dealing with a patient who is a possible suicide risk will find the **SAD PERSONS** checklist quite handy:

Sex (male or female)

Age (old or young)

Depression

Previous suicide attempts

Ethanol and other drugs

Reality testing/**R**ational thought (loss of)

Social support lacking

Organized suicide plan

No spouse

Sickness/**S**tated future intent

Signs of Mania

Medics have to **DIG FAST** to identify key symptoms of manic behaviour:

Distractibility
Indiscretion (excessive involvement
in pleasurable activities)
Grandiosity
Flight of ideas
Activity increase
Sleep deficit (decreased need for sleep)
Talkativeness (pressured speech)

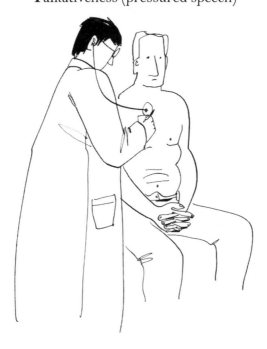

Signs of Schizophrenia

If doctors suspect a patient may have schizophrenia, they will check for **WHID**:

Withdrawn, **H**allucinations,
Inappropriate emotional response, **D**elusions

Signs of Anxiety Disorder

Your doctor will test for **MR FISC** if you're suffering from GAD—General Anxiety Disorder:

Motor tension
Restlessness
Fatigue
Irritability
Sleep disturbances
Concentration difficulty

The Heart

The signs of heart failure are ABCDE:

Acidosis, **B**lue skin, **C**old skin, **D**ilated heart,
Edema

Doctors' Shorthand

Doctors-to-be develop their sense of humour as students and refine it throughout their careers. Consequently, doctors have been known to write F BUNDY on patients' notes if the prognosis is grim:

F*ed B**ut **U**nfortunately **N**ot **D**ead **Y**et

Fever Facts

Your doctor will check the **FACTS** to diagnose influenza or just "man flu"; that is, a cold:

Fever
Aches
Chills
Tiredness
Sudden symptoms

Vitamins Are Healthy

Vitamins help maintain health. This rhyme reminds us of
the important qualities of each and every vitamin:

    Vitamin **A** keeps the cold germs away

    And tends to make meek people nervy,

    B's what you need

    When you're going to seed,

    And **C** is specific in scurvy.

    Vitamin **D** makes the bones in your knee

    Tough and hard for the service on Sunday,

    While **E** makes hens scratch

    And increases the hatch

    And brings in more profits on Monday.

    Vitamin **F** never bothers the chef

    For this vitamin never existed.

    G puts the fight in the old appetite

    And you eat all the foods that are listed.

    So now when you dine remember these lines;

    If long on this globe you will tarry.

    Just try to be good and pick out more food

    From the orchard, the garden, and dairy.

14
Lifesaving Tips

Learning and reviewing lifesaving techniques might be the best thing you ever do, so pay attention and refresh your memory regarding the many first-aid-related acronyms in existence.

The main aim of First Aid is the **3 Ps**:

Preserve life
Prevent deterioration in the patient's condition
Promote recovery

ABC is the traditional and essential way to remember what to check when administering cardiopulmonary resuscitation on a casualty:

Airways

Breathing

Circulation

Here are two groups of **3 Bs** to remember when dealing with an accident victim:

Check **B**reath **B**efore **B**lood (flow)
And then **B**lood **B**efore **B**ones

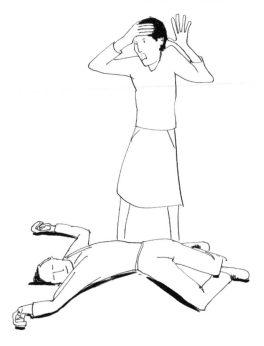

Keep calm in an emergency, and think **AMEGA**:

Assess the situation
Make the area safe
Emergency aid
Get help
Aftermath

How alert is your casualty? Check for **AVPU**:

Alert
Voice
Pain
Unconscious

Is the victim in circulatory shock? Look for **PCFATS**:

Pale
Cold and **C**lammy skin
Fast pulse
Anxious
Thirsty
Sick

Assess the injuries. Look at areas of soft tissue and bones, and think **RICE**:

Rest
Ice/**I**mmobilize
Compression
Elevation

If your victim is lucid, ask these **AMPLE** questions:

Allergies—do they have any?
Medication—are they taking any?
Past history—do they have any prior medical problems?
Last meal—what/when did they last eat?
Environment—do they know where they are?

If the injured party is in a coma, it could be caused by any of the following **MIDAS** problems:

Meningitis
Intoxication
Diabetes
Air (respiratory failure)
Subdural/**S**ubarachnoid hemorrhage

Or by **COMA**:

CO$_2$ (carbon dioxide) and **CO** (carbon monoxide) excess
Overdose: drugs, such as insulin, paracetamol, etc.
Metabolic: BSL (blood sugar level), Na+ (sodium), K+ (potassium), Mg^2+ (magnesium), urea, ammonia, etc.
Apoplexy: stroke, meningitis, encephalitis, cerebral abscess, etc.

Keep the word **FAST** in mind when assessing the condition of a possible stroke victim:

Face: is one side of the face drooping downward?
Arm: can the person raise both arms?
Speech: is the person's speech slurred or confusing;
is the person unable to speak?
Time: time is critical.
Call an ambulance immediately.

If you witness a person collapsing, what could have caused it? Think **I'VE FALLEN**:

Illness
Vestibular (balance problem)
Environmental
Feet or **F**ootwear
Alcohol and/or drugs
Low blood pressure
Low oxygen status
Ears or **E**yes
Neuropathy

Is the patient in shock? If so, he or she might be suffering from any one of the **R**egistered **N**urse **CHAMPS** range of shocks:

Respiratory
Neurogenic
Cardiogenic
Hemorrhagic
Anaphylactic
Metabolic
Psychogenic
Septic

Survival Techniques

If it's a case of personal survival out in the wilds, use extreme survival expert Ray Mears's word **STOP**:

Stop
Take inventory
Orientate
Plan

In the event of discovering a fire, think **FIRE**.

Find the fire
Inform people by shouting out
Restrict the spread of fire (*if it is safe to do so*)
Evacuate the area/**Ex**tinguish the fire
(*if it is safe to do so*)
And don't forget to **S**top, **D**rop, and **R**oll to stay clear of
the rising smoke.

Driving a Car

Mirror **S**ignal **M**aneuver is an essential phrase drummed into all student drivers, but it's one that drivers should never forget. Say it to yourself before you start, turn, change lane, reverse, and stop. It's a motorist's way of applying the "Look Before You Leap" principle.

Don't forget to buckle up, too:

Click it or Ticket

Road Safety

When learning to cross the road, children of all ages have been strongly advised to remember these life-saving lines:

Look Right, Look Left, Then Right Again
Stop, Look and Listen

You may also remember the useful public-service announcement from the 1970s, which featured people from different walks of life, saying, "Cross at the green, not in between," in many different languages. In between their statements, the announcer firmly urges:

No matter how you say it,
it always means the same thing.
Cross at the green, not in between.
It means cross at the corner,
never in the middle of the block;
don't walk until the light turns green;
always cross at corners
where motorists expect you
and where you can see them.
Cross at the green, not in between
In any language, it's a way of life.

15

The World of Work

The world of business and employment can be a cut-throat one, which is why it helps to be ahead of the game and gain an advantage over competitors whether individuals or entire companies.

Business Internet Domain Names

As with all aspects of selling yourself, choosing a name for your website is as vital as any other way of making sure people notice your business and, most important, remember it.

Here's the list that the UK Freeserve website defines as the key to success: **RAIL**

Recall   Will the name be easy to remember?

Aesthetics   How will the name look on the screen or on paper?

Impressions   First impressions always count.

Length   Keep it short and sweet. Less is definitely more.

Business Presentations

In any type of public meeting, seminar, or lecture, never forget your **ABC** and always be:

Accurate, **B**rief, and **C**lear

PPPPP

To give a good presentation, plan ahead and remember the **5 Ps**:

Proper **P**lanning **P**revents **P**oor **P**erformance.

PRIDE

Whatever line of work you're in—take **PRIDE** in what you're doing:

Personal **R**esponsibility **I**n **D**aily **E**fforts

To B or Not to B

Be **B**rave and **B**elieve; and don't be **B**oring or **B**ashful.

KISS

No matter how you earn a living, never forget to:

Keep **I**t **S**imple, **S**tupid.

The **KISS** acronym is applied to principles of business, advertising, computer operating systems to science and learning. Albert Einstein's maxim was: "Everything should be made as simple as possible, but no simpler."

SWOT Analysis

SWOT is a study of four crucial elements of a business's planning process:

Strengths, **W**eaknesses, **O**pportunities, **T**hreats

Never ASSUME Anything

Every business person knows that making assumptions is the mother of all screwups:

To assume makes an **ASS** out of **U** and **ME**.

Office Egos

In the world of employment and life in general, it's sometimes wise to keep your ego under control to avoid making enemies of at least half the population. Stick to the **FASTA** technique:

Focus on your goals, not just on yourself.
Ask for other people's opinions.
  You can learn from others.
Say thank you. Always a good idea in any situation.
Treat everyone as your equal.
  Other people know stuff that you don't.
Allow yourself to fail.
  You learn from your mistakes.

Sales Techniques

If you have something to sell, always **PLAN** in advance:

Prepare with research (don't forget your 5 Ps)
Lose time, lose all
Analyze the situation
Never just call (always have a viable reason)
  to make contact if you are making a "cold call."

During a sales pitch, meeting, or presentation, these should be your **AIMS**:

> **A**rrest the senses
> **I**nterest by questions and novelty
> **M**ove by proof and demonstration
> **S**ucceed in getting a "yes."

Think **ETC** after the pitch has been made:

> **E**valuate the outcome
> **T**each yourself and others
> **C**heck for results.

How to Interview

The first mnemonic a journalist learns is the five Ws and the H. The worst moment during an interview is when the subject gives only *yes* or *no* answers. Phrasing a question with these words gets people talking and should prevent single-word replies.

Who? **W**hen? **W**here? **W**hat? **W**hy? **H**ow?

SMART

Use this mnemonic for setting goals. It's a powerful tool for personal planning and kick-starting your career. Setting goals is all about knowing what you want to achieve and where to concentrate your efforts. You have to be **SMART**! Your daily "to do" list must be:

Specific, **M**easurable, **A**ttainable, **R**elevant, **T**ime-bound

AIDA

Advertisers need to urge people to buy their products, so they design arresting images and messages for consumers. The key principles of advertising are:

Attract **A**ttention—"Look at that!"
Arouse **I**nterest—"Mmm, that looks interesting!"
Create **D**esire—"I want it!"
Urge **A**ction—"Now!"

Job Interview Techniques

Preparing for meetings is vital in business, and job interviews are possibly the most important meetings in your business life. Your aim at an interview is to sell yourself—you are the product. Hence the need for the **STAR** system:

Situation—Describe your previous experience regarding situations that you have managed successfully.

TAsk—Give details of exactly how you managed the situation. What was your contribution to the task? A tip from the professionals—don't make it up, and don't exaggerate, because you'll be found out!

Result—Congratulations. You're hired!

16

Other Favourites

Champagne Bottles

Name	Capacity	No. of Bottles
Quarter	187.5 mL	—
Half-bottle	375 mL	—
Bottle	750 mL	1
Magnum	1.5 L	2
Jeroboam	3 L	4
Rehoboam	4.5 L	6
Methuselah	6 L	8
Salmanazar	9 L	12
Balthazar	12 L	16
Nebuchadnezzar	15 L	20

One way to recall the names of different-sized bottles of champagne is to think of a detective in the company of some ancient men:

Magnum—1980s TV private detective
(or gun)

Jeroboam—Founder and first king of Israel,
931–910 BC
Rehoboam—Son of Solomon, king of Judah,
922–908 BC
Methuselah—Biblical patriarch who lived
to the age of 969
Salmanazar—King of Assyria, 859–824 BC
Balthazar—Son of Nabonide, Regent of Babylon, 539 BC
Nebuchadnezzar—King of Babylon, 605–562 BC

Otherwise this rude mnemonic could jog your memory:

My **J**oanna **R**eally **M**akes **S**plendid **B**urping **N**oises.

Alcohol Tips

Few people need tips on drinking alcohol, but some
drinkers swear by the advice offered in this rhyme:

> Beer on whisky? Very risky!
> Whisky on beer, never fear . . .

Mixing drinks isn't a wise thing to do, but the warning
quote below says it succinctly and honestly:

> Never mix grape with the grain.

Steering a Boat

If you find yourself behind the wheel of a boat, it helps to
recall which side of the boat is port (the left side with red
lights) and starboard (the right side with green lights).
Fortunately, there are several ways to jog one's memory:

> PORT has four letters and so has LEFT.
>
> P (port) comes before S (starboard) in the alphabet,
> as L (left) comes before R (right).
>
> PORT wine should be LEFT alone when it is RED
> (therefore starboard is RIGHT).
>
> There's a little RED PORT LEFT in the bottle.

Five Sailing Essentials

This handy phrase reminds the crew of a boat of the "Five Essentials" of sailing:

Can The Boat Sail Correctly?

Course to steer—the course might be a particular bearing (as, say, 250 degrees) or at a particular angle to the apparent wind.

Trim—the fore and aft balance of the boat. The movable ballast on the boat is of course the crew, and the aim is to achieve an even keel.

Balance—the port and starboard balance. This is also about adjusting the weight inboard or outboard.

Sail—this is to ensure the sails are set correctly until they fill with wind. The front edge, or luff, of the sail should be in line with the wind.

Centreboard—if the boat has a movable centreboard, it should be lowered when sailing close to the wind. It is raised on a downwind course to reduce drag.

Left and Right

An oft-heard criticism of some organizations is that the right hand doesn't know what the left hand is doing, which is a bit of a problem if you can't even tell the difference.

A quick physical mnemonic you can use to remember is to place your left-hand palm down, rotate your left thumb 90 degrees clockwise so that the forefinger and thumb make the shape of L for Left.

Interest Rates

Every city slicker knows this one:

> When rates are low
> Stocks will grow.
> When rates are high
> Stocks will die.

A Game of Bridge

The order of suits from highest to lowest are:

Spades, **H**earts, **D**iamonds, **C**lubs

If the order of suits just won't stick in your mind, try remembering the following fact:

Sally **H**as **D**irty **C**hildren.

Basic DIY Techniques

So you've found the screwdriver and climbed the ladder, but you don't know which way to turn the screw because it was secured so tightly the last time round? This invaluable expression will guarantee that you don't waste precious minutes trying to unscrew a screw the wrong way:

> Righty-tighty,
> Lefty-loosey.

Or how about:

> Right on; left off.

And the mantra of every smart woodworker:

> Measure twice,
> Cut once.

The Great Outdoors

If you're invited on a huntin', shootin' and fishin' weekend with the boss, remember the following acronym: **BRASS**.

Breathe, **R**elax, **A**im, **S**ight, **S**queeze

By keeping this sequence in mind, it might help you to shoot a rifle without missing your targets by a mile, or at least make you look like you know what you're doing .. . .

Setting a Table

When preparing for your next holiday or dinner party, remember that items to the left of the plate have EVEN letters, like the word LEFT (4): FORK (4) and NAPKIN (6). Items to the right of the plate have ODD letters, like the word RIGHT (5): KNIFE (5), SPOON (5), GLASS (5).

Helpful Mnemonics Websites

———

www.fun-with-words.com/mnem_example.html

en.wikiquote.org/wiki/List_of_mnemonics

www.learningassistance.com/2006/january/mnemonics.html

teachers.net/gazette/AUG00/poll.html

psych.athabascau.ca/html/Psych355/Exp/mnemonics.shtml?sso=true

www.k8accesscenter.org/training_resources/Mnemonics.asp

www.ababasoft.com/mnemonic/tech01.htm

members.tripod.com/~forgetknot

www.spellingsociety.org/news/media/poems.php

www.papernapkin.com/imagine/index.html

www.papernapkin.com/atomic/_table.html

www.celsius-to-fahrenheit.com